OF
FAITH
AND
REASON

OF
FAITH
AND
REASON

EIGHTY EVIDENCES SUPPORTING
THE PROPHET
Joseph Smith

Michael R. Ash

CFI
Springville, Utah

ISBN 13: 978-1-59955-231-6

Published by CFI, an imprint of Cedar Fort, Inc., 2373 W. 700 S., Springville, UT 84663
Distributed by Cedar Fort, Inc., www.cedarfort.com

LIBRARY OF CONGRESS CATALOGING-IN-PUBLICATION DATA
Ash, Michael R.
  Of Faith and Reason: eighty evidences supporting the prophet Joseph Smith / Michael R. Ash.
    p. cm.
  Includes bibliographical references (p.   ).
  ISBN 978-1-59955-231-6
  1. Smith, Joseph, 1805-1844. I. Title.
  BX8695.S6A776 2009
  289.3092--dc22
                              2008035023

Cover design by Angela D. Olsen
Cover design © 2008 by Lyle Mortimer
Edited and typeset by Melissa J. Caldwell

Printed in the United States of America

10 9 8 7 6 5 4 3 2 1

Printed on acid-free paper

For my best friend—my wife

CONTENTS

Introduction   **xi**

Joseph Smith
  1. A Prophet's Birth from Noble Heritage   **3**
  2. A Miracle Operation   **4**
  3. Joseph Smith's Name Known Worldwide   **7**

Book of Mormon
  4. Joseph Smith Retrieved Real Artifacts from Moroni's
     Stone Box   **13**
  5. Book of Mormon Witnesses   **15**
  6. Time of Translation   **20**
  7. Textual Consistency   **20**
  8. Evidence for Dictation   **22**
  9. Book of Mormon Politics Unlike Joseph Smith's   **26**

Book of Mormon Language
  10. Word Prints   **31**
  11. Chiasmus   **32**
  12. If/And Conditional Sentences   **34**
  13. Hebraisms   **35**
  14. The "Rent" Garment, Part 1   **37**

15. "It Came to Pass," Part 1   **38**

16. "Reformed Egyptian"   **38**

17. The Name "Nephi"   **40**

18. The Name "Sariah"   **40**

19. The Names "Paanchi" and "Pahoran"   **41**

20. Alma as a Male Name   **41**

21. Mulek, Son of Zedekiah   **42**

22. Deseret and Bees   **43**

23. More Names   **43**

24. "Without a Cause"   **45**

Book of Mormon: Journey through the Old World

25. Axial Period   **51**

26. Laban and His "Fifty"   **51**

27. Killing Laban and the Oath of Zoram   **52**

28. Unknown Arabia   **53**

29. Trails   **54**

30. Trail Names   **54**

31. Nephi's Bow   **55**

32. Tree of Life, Part 1   **56**

33. Nephi and His Asherah   **58**

34. The Liahona   **61**

35. Nahom   **62**

36. Raw Meat   **63**

37. Bountiful   **65**

38. Ancient Shipbuilding   **66**

39. Transoceanic Crossings   **67**

Book of Mormon: Other Old World Evidences

40. Angels and Books   **75**

41. Jared's Ships   **75**

42. Chopping Down the Execution Tree   **78**

43. The "Rent" Garment, Part 2   **78**

44. Hidden Records   **79**

45. Thieves and Robbers   **81**
46. Nephite Money   **81**
47. Sheum   **83**
48. Land of Jerusalem   **83**
49. Temple Outside of Jerusalem   **85**
50. Metal Plates and Stone Boxes   **86**
51. Doubled, Sealed Documents   **88**
52. Olive Culture   **89**
53. King Benjamin's Speech   **92**
54. Disarming Ammon   **94**
55. Columbus   **94**

Book of Mormon: New World Evidences
56. Book of Mormon Geography   **101**
57. Unknown New World   **104**
58. Mesoamerican Cultures   **105**
59. The Marketplace   **107**
60. New World Writings   **108**
61. "It Came to Pass," Part 2   **109**
62. Tumbaga   **110**
63. New World Temples and Towers   **113**
64. Mesoamerican Warfare   **114**
65. Seasonality of Warfare   **116**
66. Cement   **118**
67. Barley   **119**
68. List of Book of Mormon Items   **120**
69. Tree of Life, Part 2   **121**
70. Uto-Aztecan Language   **122**
71. Earthquakes and Volcanoes   **123**
72. Four Hundred Year Baktun   **125**
73. Mesoamerican Demographic and History Cycles   **126**

Book of Abraham
74. Ur and Olishem   **133**

75. Heliocentric Universe   **133**
76. More Book of Abraham Evidences   **135**

Doctrine

77. The Apostasy   **141**
78. Plain and Precious Parts   **143**
79. A Closed Canon   **146**
80. The Restoration   **146**
81. Premortal Existence   **147**
82. Council in Heaven   **148**
83. Secret Teachings among the Apostles   **149**
84. Sacred Vestments   **152**
85. Salvation for the Dead   **156**
86. Degrees of Glory   **160**
87. Deification   **161**
88. Word of Wisdom   **164**
89. Fruits of Education   **171**

Conclusion   **179**
Appendix   **181**
About the Author   **191**

INTRODUCTION

*M*ormonism," writes one LDS-critical author, "would gain a measure of respectability if only some credible evidence could be found to support at least one of Joseph Smith's claims."[1] Another detractor asserts that if there was substantial evidence supporting LDS beliefs, then Mormonism "would deserve the prayerful investigation of every man and woman in the world."[2] We would certainly agree. Paul said, "Prove all things; hold fast that which is good" (1 Thessalonians 5:21).

Are there solid secular evidences for Joseph Smith's prophetic abilities, the antiquity of the scriptures he translated, and the doctrines he restored? The answer is a resounding "Yes!" Fortunately, we live in a day of advanced LDS scholarship and rapidly accumulating evidences that support LDS faith claims. Dozens of scholars have contributed to the study of Joseph Smith and the unique scriptures he was instrumental in restoring.

Do these evidences translate into proof? To answer, we might ask another question—is there secular "proof" for the existence of God, the Resurrection, or the Atonement? The answer, of course, is no.

Why not? Why is there no proof for the existence of God? Why didn't God leave the golden plates for everyone to see so we would *know* that the Book of Mormon is true? Free will requires alternative choices. Each choice must offer some attraction. If, for example, there were overwhelming, intellectually decisive evidence for the existence of God, most rational people would be compelled to accept Him. This would frustrate the principle of faith by not allowing us to freely follow our hearts and true desires. We would, in effect, be subject to the plan proposed by Satan in the premortal existence—we would be coerced to comply with God's laws and return to Him. Likewise, if there were massive archaeological support for the Book of Mormon, faith would be unnecessary in accepting Joseph Smith or Mormonism, and God's plan would be frustrated.

Faith—which entails humility and a heart aligned with the teachings of the Savior—is necessary for true conversion. "No man can say that Jesus is the Lord," wrote Paul, "but by the Holy Ghost" (1 Corinthians 12:3). John likewise explained that "the testimony of Jesus is the spirit of prophecy" (Revelation 19:10). The same principle applies to a belief in the Restored Gospel. B. H. Roberts once observed, "The chief source of evidence for the truth of the Book of Mormon" is a witness from the Spirit. "All other evidence is secondary."[3] Likewise, the late Hugh Nibley explained, "Though archaeology may conceivably confirm the existence of a prophet (though it has never yet done so), it can never prove or disprove the visions that make the prophet a significant figure."[4]

If faith is necessary for spiritual conversion, then why even bother with secular evidences? Mormonism teaches that in the search for truth, we are to use both our intellects as well as our spirits. "Each of us," said Elder Boyd K. Packer, "must accommodate the mixture of reason and revelation in our lives. The gospel not only permits but *requires* it."[5] When Oliver Cowdery attempted to translate the Book of Mormon, he failed. The Lord told him why:

> Behold, you have not understood; you have supposed that I would give it unto you, when you took no thought save it was to ask me.
>
> But, behold, I say unto you, that you must study it out in your mind; then you must ask me if it be right, and if it is right I will cause that your bosom shall burn within you; therefore, you shall feel that it is right. (D&C 9:7–8)

Both our hearts and are minds must be utilized in searching for truth. LDS scholar John Welch used the following analogy: "In the bicycle-built-for-two metaphor, the relationship between reason and revelation is likened to two riders on a tandem bicycle. When both riders pedal together, the bicycle (the search for truth) moves ahead more rapidly. Each rider must work, or the other must bear a heavy and perhaps exhausting burden; but only one (that is faith) can steer and determine where the bicycle will go, although the other (reason) can do some backseat driving."[6]

In an 1832 revelation to Joseph Smith, the Lord explained that since "all have not faith" that we should "seek . . . diligently . . . words of wisdom" from the "best books"—that we should "seek learning even by study and also by faith" (D&C 88:118). Secular evidences can't replace a spiritual witness, but they can support a testimony, and they can provide an atmosphere where a spiritual witness can flourish. President Gordon B. Hinckley once said that while the truth of the Book of Mormon ultimately rests in the spiritual realm, "archaeology or anthropology" may prove "helpful to some" in confirming their religious convictions.[7]

In science, validity of a theory or proposition is typically determined by how well the theory accounts for all the evidence as well as how well it explains counter-evidences or anomalies (and all propositions have at least some anomalies). In the case of Mormon studies, the anomalies would be the theories and claims of critics and detractors. Most of those arguments have been answered by LDS apologists (*apologetics* means to "defend one's faith"). LDS apologetic responses, for example, are found in the writings of FAIR (the Foundation for Apologetic Information and Research)—a grass roots all-volunteer organization that was created to defend LDS beliefs. While criticisms will never disappear, some of the criticisms from Joseph Smith's day have vanished as newer evidence has rendered such arguments invalid. Throughout this book, for example, I'll quote Mormon critics to demonstrate that many of the unique things taught by Joseph Smith were once ridiculed but now have turned into "hits" for his prophetic abilities. When we examine those things which Joseph Smith claims came from God, we find that the proposition proposed by Joseph Smith—that he was an instrument in the restoration of the Lord's Church—fits all of the evidence better than any other theory.

Hugh Nibley was probably the best known LDS scholar for the current generation of Latter-day Saints. He dug both deep and wide and peeked into crevices that are now being opened by younger scholars. For much of the latter half of the twentieth century, he researched the answers to questions that most members had never even thought of asking. He gave lectures and produced numerous articles and books and he made us realize that the Book of Mormon fits the Old World milieu from which it claims to have originally derived.

Traversing the path paved by Nibley and other earlier LDS scholars are a new group of scholars. Some work at Brigham Young University, others work at different universities or in other professions. Most of these modern pundits have published research with FARMS (The Foundation for Ancient Research and Mormon Studies)—part of the Neal A. Maxwell Institute for Religious Scholarship at BYU. FARMS has motivated LDS scholarship like never before and the result has been an explosion in research—primarily on the Book of Mormon and Book of Abraham. Many scholars who contribute to FARMS are experts in history, archaeology, anthropology, linguistics, Egyptology, Mesoamerican Archaeology and Ethnohistory, as well as Ancient Near Eastern studies and early Judaeo-Christian traditions.

Utilizing the professional tools of the trade, LDS scholars have applied their expertise to Mormon issues, thereby blessing us with a greater understanding of Joseph Smith and the things he restored. What has emerged from such research is a growing corpus of evidence that Joseph Smith was a prophet and that the Book of Mormon and Book of Abraham are based on authentic ancient texts. It's now demonstrable that Joseph made numerous bulls-eye "hits" that he couldn't have likely known in the early 1800s. Such evidential support allows the option of belief versus disbelief to hang in a balance—thereby making a true choice possible.

While Nibley's name is probably the most familiar to today's Latter-day Saints, it seems (from my own anecdotal experiences) that relatively few members have actually read his writings. FAIR—the apologetics group which generates hundreds of Internet articles defending LDS beliefs (and has published my own apologetic book, *Shaken Faith Syndrome*)—has been around for over a decade yet remains virtually unknown to most Mormons. Likewise, FARMS—which came into existence in 1979 and has produced hundreds of books, journals, and other publications—is either unfamiliar to most members, or only superficially familiar. This should not be surprising since most people prefer fiction over non-fiction, and TV, Internet, sports, and so forth, over reading educational material of any kind. A 2002 survey, for instance, found that the average US adult spends about six times more time watching TV than reading books.[8] Unfortunately, this seems to be the case with members of the Church as well. For some people, non-fiction—and especially scholarly writings—can be boring or hard to understand. Although LDS scholarship has been amassing evidence for the authenticity of the Restoration for over half a century—and a significant portion just within the last three decades—most members are completely unaware of these exciting discoveries.

The purpose of this book is to share some of the evidences for the prophetic abilities of Joseph Smith, the antiquity of many unique LDS doctrines and practices, and the fascinating support for the authenticity of the LDS scriptures. While I rely on the research of top LDS scholars, the data is presented in short snippets that should make it easier to both read and digest. For those whose appetites are teased by the summaries in this book, the endnotes will lead to more in-depth material. Because the doctrinal portion of this book draws upon material from ancient Jewish and Christian writings that were generally unknown to the people of Joseph Smith's day and times, the appendix includes a "Primer on Ancient Documents" that offers a guide to the fascinating discovery, categorization, and importance of these ancient texts.

NOTES

1. Ed Decker and Dave Hunt, *The God Makers* (Oregon: Harvest House Publishers, 1984), 87.

2. William J. Whalen, *The Latter-day Saints in the Modern Day World* (University of Notre Dame Press, 1964), 37.

3. B. H. Roberts, *New Witnesses for God,* 3 vols. (Salt Lake City, UT: Deseret Book, 1909), 2: vi–vii.

4. Hugh Nibley, *Old Testament and Related Studies* (Salt Lake City, UT: Deseret Book; Provo, UT: FARMS, 1986), 33.

5. Boyd K. Packer, "I Say unto You, Be One," *Brigham Young University*

1990–91 Speeches (Provo, UT: Brigham Young University, 1991), 8.

6. John W. Welch, "The Power of Evidence in the Nurturing of Faith," *Nurturing Faith through the Book of Mormon: the 24th Annual Sidney B. Sperry Symposium* (Salt Lake City, UT: Deseret Book, 1995), 151.

7. Gordon B. Hinckley, "Four Cornerstones of Faith," *Ensign,* Feb. 2004, 6.

8. "Reading at Risk: A Survey of Literary Reading in America," National Endowment for the Arts, Research Division Report #46 (June 2004), xi; available on-line at http://arts.endow.gov/pub/readingatrisk.pdf (accessed 15 May 2008).

Joseph Smith

1. A Prophet's Birth from Noble Heritage

The setting was early frontier America, January 24, 1796. Only twenty years had passed since the United States had declared her independence when Joseph Smith Sr., the future father of Joseph Smith Jr., married Lucy Mack at Tunbridge, Vermont. Joseph Sr. was born at Topsfield, Massachusetts, July 12, 1771, and his wife, Lucy, was born four days after the signing of the Declaration of Independence, while her father was gone to war.

Both Joseph Sr. and Lucy came from a line of worthy ancestors. Some of their progenitors were patriots, pioneers, and ministers. Seven were pilgrims who sailed on the Mayflower, and three of the seven signed the Mayflower Compact.

One of Lucy's ancestors was John Lathrop, a former minister of the Church of England in the early seventeenth century, who allied himself with an independent religious body when he no longer approved of the church government. For eight years Lathrop and his congregation met secretly in London until they were finally caught and arrested. Two years later all were released except Lathrop. During his continuing imprisonment, Lathrop's wife became fatally ill, and he was allowed to visit his wife in her dying moments. Following her death, however, Lathrop was forced to return to jail, leaving his children as orphans. He pleaded with the bishop for the sake of his children and was finally released. Shortly thereafter, Lathrop and his children sailed to America where he became a leader in church affairs.

A year after Joseph Sr. and Lucy wed, they delivered their first child, an unnamed daughter, who died shortly after birth. The following year, on February 11, 1798, Joseph and Lucy had a boy whom they named Alvin. Two more children were born to the Smiths while living in Tunbridge; Hyrum on February 9, 1800, and Sophronia on May 16, 1803. The Smiths then rented out their farm in Tunbridge and moved to Randolph to open a mercantile establishment where they attempted to sell ginseng. But things didn't go as planned. The local dealer's crooked son ran off with the Smith's profits and left them in debt for eighteen hundred dollars. They were forced to sell their farm for eight hundred dollars—only half its assessed value—and Lucy gave up her wedding present of one thousand dollars so that they might be free from debt.[1]

Having sold the farm, the Smiths moved again: first to Royalton, and then a few months later to Sharon, Vermont, where Joseph purchased a farm from Lucy's father, Solomon Mack. During the summer Joseph Sr. cultivated the farm and during the winter he taught school. Gradually, their financial circumstances became more comfortable.

The year was now 1805. Twenty-nine years had passed since America had declared her independence from England, and only twenty-two years had lapsed since the Revolutionary War had formally ended. The Bill of Rights had been in force for only fourteen years, and George Washington had died just six years earlier, two years after leaving the office of president. Thomas Jefferson was serving as president of the United States—which consisted of only seventeen of our current fifty states—and two years previous, President Jefferson had made the Louisiana Purchase. The first steam vehicle on rails had been attempted just one year earlier, and it would still be another sixty-eight years before the invention of barbed wire. On December 23 in Sharon, Vermont, Joseph Smith Jr. (the fifth child of an eventual eleven) was born to the Smiths.

2. A Miracle Operation

Most Latter-day Saints are familiar with the basic story of Joseph's childhood leg operation, but they may not know how blessed he was to have the right doctor at the right time.

In 1812 the Smiths moved to Lebanon, New Hampshire, and one

year later all the children were hit with Typhus fever. Sophronia, the oldest daughter, was on the verge of death and the Smith's believed that her life was spared due their prayers. Eight-year-old Joseph was also sick but seemed to recover until he developed a large painful fever sore near his shoulder. After two weeks of suffering, a doctor came to the house and lanced the sore. The pain went away in his shoulder but reappeared in his leg.

For several more weeks, Joseph suffered in excruciating, almost unbearable, pain. To ease the suffering, his mother Lucy and his brother Hyrum would take turns squeezing Joseph leg in their hands. Finally a doctor cut the sore leg to the bone, relieving the pressure and the agony. When his leg began to heal, however, the pain returned. Eventually, a group of doctors gathered and concluded that the bone was so affected that amputation was probably necessary to save his life. Lucy overheard them discussing an experimental procedure wherein the infected bone could be cut from the leg, and she pleaded with them to try this risky operation instead.

Today we know that Joseph likely suffered from osteomyelitis, a disorder that causes long segments of the bony shaft to die and then become encased by new bone growing over the dead layer. Inevitably, the dead bone separates and lies in the center of an abscess cavity, draining continuously or spreading infection to other parts of the body—eventually resulting in death. Today, such a problem can be resolved with a simple operation. In early nineteenth century America, however, the typical cure for osteomyelitis was amputation because there were no surgeons as we understand "surgeons" today. Those physicians who practiced surgery did so out of necessity rather than training. In fact, few medical practitioners in Jacksonian America had ever attended medical school, and in 1813 New England there was not a single institution that could be called a hospital.[2]

Consenting to the desires of both Joseph and Lucy, the doctors agreed to attempt the experimental procedure. They suggested strapping Joseph to his bed, but Joseph objected, claiming that he could bear the operation better unbound. The surgeon then offered Joseph some brandy or wine to lessen the pain. Joseph refused, requesting instead that his father hold him and that his mother leave the room. Lucy had walked several hundred yards from the house to be out of hearing range when the surgeons began boring into Joseph's leg, breaking off pieces of bone with forceps. She wrote of the experience:

> When they broke off the first piece [of bone], Joseph screamed out so loudly, that I could not forbear running to him. On my entering the room he cried out, "Oh, mother, go back, go back; I do not want you to come in—I will try to tough it out, if you will go away."
>
> When the third piece was taken away, I burst into the room again—and oh, my God! What a spectacle for a mother's eye! The wound torn open, the blood still gushing from it, and the bed literally covered with blood. Joseph was as pale as a corpse, and large drops of sweat were rolling down his face, whilst upon every feature was depicted the utmost agony![3]

Lucy was forced from the room and detained until the operation was over. The operation was a success and Joseph slowly began to recover. It's significant to point out that this was the year 1813—seventy-six years before the discovery of aspirin, fifty-four years before Joseph Lister published his articles on the antiseptic treatment of wounds, ninety-two years before the development of iodine, seventy years before sterilized gowns and caps were introduced into operating rooms, and ninety-three years before Willis MacDonald suggested that surgeons wash their hands before operating to reduce the chance of infection.[4]

Arthur E. Hertzler, a physician who grew up in the late eighteen hundreds, recorded his memories of nineteenth century medical practices. In the rural districts—such as where the Smiths lived—operations were "practically unknown." Hertzler wrote,

> In the first operation I witnessed the surgeon threaded the needles with silk and then stuck them in his lapel of his coat so as to have them readily accessible when needed. He held the knife in his teeth when not in actual use.
>
> Injuries which today seem comparatively trivial were treated by amputation. . . . The reason for such radical measures was that because of suppuration the surgeon, usually called from a distance, found amputation the most practical measure. . . . The experience was that if amputation was not done death from infection would most likely follow, an end not obviated, however, in many cases by amputation, because the wound made by the amputation often became infected and killed the patient.[5]

Since anesthesia and chloroform would remain unknown until 1846 and 1872 (thirty-three years and fifty-nine years after Joseph's operation), most patients drank whisky and perhaps prayed while being sutured. When a limb had to be amputated, the mark of a good surgeon was speed. One surgeon in the Civil War, for example, cut a leg off at the thigh in forty seconds (from the time of the initial incision until the severed limb hit the floor).[6]

The surgery performed on young Joseph was not widely known or even extensively suggested until the late 1800s and wasn't standardized until after World War I. So how did Joseph get such an odd operation in 1813? According to the research of Dr. LeRoy Wirthlin, a Dr. Nathan Smith (no relation to Joseph) was the surgeon who performed Joseph's operation. Perhaps not coincidentally, Dr. Smith had more experience with osteomyelitis than anyone one else in the country, and his success rate was good. Surprisingly, after his death, his work and results were not repeated until the early twentieth century.

Dr. Smith's work was generations ahead of his time, and he was the only physician in the United States in 1813 who had the expertise to successfully deal with Joseph's bone disease. If Joseph Smith had lived anywhere else or perhaps a few decades earlier or later, he would have lost his leg. Although this experimental and rare operation left Joseph on crutches for three years (and gave him a slight limp for the rest of his life), the procedure saved his leg and perhaps his life.

3. Joseph Smith's Name Known Worldwide

On the twenty-first of September, 1823, after retiring to bed, Joseph prayed that he might know his standing before God. While praying, a light appeared in his room, followed by a personage clothed in white. The messenger identified himself as Moroni and said that God had a work for Joseph, that his name would be had for good and evil among all nations, kindreds, and tongues, and that it should be both good and evil spoken of among all people (Joseph Smith—History 1:32–33). This prophecy was made in 1823, seven years before the Book of Mormon was published and the Church organized. What would be the chances of such a prophecy reaching fruition? What are the statistical odds that

Joseph Smith would have correctly guessed that his name would be known for "good and evil" throughout the world?

Church membership has doubled every fifteen years and now has over thirteen million members. While the LDS religion is the fourth largest church in the United States,[7] most of its members now live outside of this country. There are wards or branches in 162 different countries and over 130 temples throughout the world—one on every continent except Antarctica. This is quite an achievement for a religion which the critics of Joseph Smith's day predicted would fizzle out after the Prophet's death. Thomas Ford, who was governor of Illinois from 1842 to 1846 and participated in the events leading to Joseph's martyrdom, said: "Joe Smith [was] the most successful imposter in modern times; a man who, though ignorant and coarse, . . . [was] fitted for temporary success, but . . . never could succeed in establishing a system of policy which looked to permanent success in the future."[8]

Governor Ford was wrong, but the young Joseph was right. Where will you find a more controversial figure than Joseph Smith? Over one hundred and fifty years after he told his story, the controversy goes on. Moroni's prophecy has truly been fulfilled.

NOTES

1. Ivan J. Barrett, *Joseph Smith and the Restoration* (Provo, Utah: Brigham Young University Press, 1973), 23–31.

2. See LeRoy S. Wirthlin, "Nathan Smith (1762–1828) Surgical Consultant to Joseph Smith," *BYU Studies* (Spring 1977) 17:3, 319; LeRoy S. Wirthlin, "Joseph Smith's Surgeon," *Ensign,* Mar. 1978, 59–61; and LeRoy S. Wirthlin, "Joseph Smith's Boyhood Operation: An 1813 Surgical Success," *BYU Studies* 21, no. 2 (Spring 1981): 131.

3. Lucy Mack Smith, *History of Joseph Smith by His Mother Lucy Mack Smith* (Salt Lake City, UT: Bookcraft), 57–58.

4. Richard H. Meade, An Introduction to the History of General Surgery (Philadelphia: W. B. Saunders Co., 1968), 32–33.

5. Arthur E. Hertzler, *The Horse and Buggy Doctor* (NY: Harper and Brothers, 1938), 6–9.

6. Ibid., 8.

7. "Mormon Population," at http://www.mormonwiki.com/Mormon_ Population (accessed 7 July 2008).

8. Thomas Ford, *History of Illinois* (New York: Ivison and Phinney; Chicago: S.C. Griggs & Co., 1854), 354–55.

Book of Mormon

4. Joseph Smith Retrieved Real Artifacts from Moroni's Stone Box

Joseph claimed that the angel Moroni lead him to golden plates engraved with the sacred record of a forgotten people. If Joseph was delusional, it would have been hard to get witnesses to testify that they had seen the plates unless they participated in his delusion or were liars. The Book of Mormon Witnesses will be discussed in section 5, while this section will explore some of the evidences that Joseph had real, physical, heavy metal plates.

Before Joseph showed the plates (under divine direction) to the Book of Mormon Witnesses, other family members were able to heft and feel the plates, although they were not allowed to see them. Joseph's brother William, for example, said that he had "handled" and "hefted" the plates while they were wrapped in a frock. He estimated that they weighed about sixty pounds and he could feel that "they were fastened together by rings running through the back."[1] He could feel and raise the individual leaves.[2]

Joseph's mother, Lucy, also felt the plates and observed that they were "all connected by a ring which passes through a hole at the end of each plate."[3] While cleaning the house, Emma (Joseph's wife), had to clean around the plates. She wrote: "The plates often lay on the table without any attempt at concealment, wrapped in a small linen table cloth, which I had given him to fold them in. I once felt of the plates as they thus lay on the table, tracing their outline and shape. They seemed to be pliable like thick paper, and would rustle with a metallic sound when the edges were moved by the thumb, as one does sometimes thumb the edges of a book."[4]

Joseph's sister Katherine was only fourteen when Joseph brought home the plates, and she felt and hefted them through a cloth. Once, while housecleaning, she lifted the wrapped plates and said they were heavy. She also rubbed her fingers along the edge of the plates and felt that they were separate metal plates that tinkled as her fingers passed over them.[5]

Likewise, Joseph's younger brother William said that he was allowed to feel the plates in a pillowcase and could tell that they were real and heavy.

It is nearly beyond dispute that Joseph had some sort of metal plates in his possession (and eleven other witnesses—who will be discussed later—saw the uncovered golden plates). Logically, it makes more sense that Joseph had some sort of metal plates than it is to believe that all those who handled the plates were liars or deluded. But what if the plates were forged from tin or lead—or some other lesser metal—and painted to look like gold?

Before Martin Harris was called to be one of the Three Witnesses ,he hefted a box with the plates inside. There was something heavy and dense within the box, he noted. It was either gold or lead and, he added, "I knew that Joseph had not credit enough to buy so much lead."[6] The Smith's were too poor to even afford that much tin. Even if Joseph had the money, however, someone would have had to purchase, fashion, paint, and engrave the tin plates—all without getting busted by some witness to the process or some clerk who recalled selling the tin or paint to Joseph Smith or a cohort.

Finally, it's significant to point out that other items—in addition to the plates—were retrieved from the stone box and handled by witnesses. Joseph's mother, Lucy, for instance, examined the Nephite Interpreters (the Urim and Thummin) and said that it "consisted of two smooth, three-cornered diamonds set in glass, and the glasses were set in silver bows, which were connected with each other in much the same way as old fashioned spectacles."[7] She also examined the breastplate.

It was wrapped in a thin muslin handkerchief, so thin that I could feel its proportions without any difficulty.

It was concave on one side and convex on the other, and extended from the neck downwards, as far as the centre of the stomach of a man of extraordinary size. It had four straps of the same material, for the purpose of fastening it to the breast, two of which ran back to go over the shoulders, and the other two were designed to fasten to the hips. They were just the width of two of my fingers (for I measured them), and they had holes in the ends of them, to be convenient in fastening.[8]

None of this fits with a theory that proposes delusion or a con. Manufacturing such items would have been cost prohibitive and would have been more valuable in raw materials and labor than any money Joseph hoped to make from a book that had been denounced and boycotted before it was even published.

It should also be noted that Joseph's family believed him immediately. Joseph's younger brother William said that they never doubted his word for one minute and that "Joseph was a truthful boy."[9] His father and mother believed Joseph because of his integrity—he was not one to tell tall tales or lies. When Joseph first called the family together to tell them of his visitation by the angel Moroni, "The whole family were melted to tears," remembers William. They "believed all he said." Because of Joseph's good "character and disposition," they knew he was "incapable of . . . giving utterance to anything but the truth."[10]

5. Book of Mormon Witnesses

In the front of every copy of the Book of Mormon are the testimonies of the Book of Mormon Witnesses. Oliver Cowdery, David Whitmer, and Martin Harris signed a statement testifying that an angel of God showed them the plates and that they heard the voice of the Lord telling them that the record which Joseph translated is true.

Eight other witnesses signed a statement testifying that Joseph had shown them physical plates (there was no angel and no voice from heaven), and that the plates were engraved with curious characters.

None of these eleven witnesses ever denied their testimonies. The possibility that the witnesses were lying becomes extremely remote when we realize that nearly all of the witnesses suffered hardship and persecution for testifying of their experiences, as well as the fact that all of the Three Witnesses and some of the Eight Witnesses left the Church—some never returned. If they were lying, chances are that at least one of the estranged witnesses—in a moment of irate rage—would have claimed that he had been conned by Joseph Smith and that the events did not really happen as recorded.

Oliver Cowdery, who served as scribe for most of the Book of Mormon translation, left the Church for a number of years. During his separation from the Saints, however, he continued to maintain the truth of those things to which he testified. Not long after returning to the Church, he contracted tuberculosis. His dying breaths were spent testifying of the truthfulness of the Book of Mormon. Lucy P. Young, his half sister, was—with other family and friends—at Oliver's bedside just before his death. She heard him testify to those present that if they would live according to the teachings in the Book of Mormon, they would meet again in heaven.[11]

Martin Harris also left the Church for a number of years. Not once, however, did he deny his testimony. Once, for example, some old acquaintances got Martin drunk on wine—hoping to get him to spill the real story about the golden plates. After Martin was tipsy, they asked him about his claims.

" 'Now, Martin, do you really believe that you did see an angel, when you were awake?' 'No,' said Martin, 'I do not believe it.' The crowd were delighted, but soon a different feeling prevailed, as Martin true to his trust, said, 'Gentlemen, what I have said is true, from the fact that my belief is swallowed up in knowledge; for I want to say to you that as the Lord lives I do know that I stood with the Prophet Joseph Smith in the presence of the angel, and it was in the brightness of day.' "[12]

Like Oliver Cowdery, Martin Harris bore his testimony while on his deathbed. Martin's highly practical neighbor, George Godfrey, deliberately waited for a semiconscious moment to suggest that Martin's testimony was possibly based on deception. Martin was so feeble that he didn't recognize Godfrey when his neighbor asked if perhaps Martin had been deceived into thinking he had seen the plates. Godfrey recorded the vigorous response:

The Book of Mormon is no fake. I know what I know. I have seen what I have seen and I have heard what I have heard. I have seen the gold plates from which the Book of Mormon is written. An angel appeared to me and others and testified to the truthfulness of the record, and had I been willing to have perjured myself and sworn falsely to the testimony I now bear I could have been a rich man, but I could not have testified other than I have done and am now doing for these things are true.[13]

The last of the Three Witnesses, David Whitmer, left the Church and never returned. For fifty years he lived outside of the Church, during which time he granted over seventy interviews. Although he remained bitter over the way he felt he had been treated by some of the Latter-day Saints, he continued to affirm the veracity of his testimony. The people of Richmond, Missouri, where David lived, knew him as honest and trustworthy, whose character was of the highest integrity and without blemish.

LDS scholar Richard L. Anderson tells how one anti-Mormon gave a lecture in Richmond, branding David as disreputable because of his involvement in Mormonism. The local non-Mormon newspaper responded with "a spirited front-page editorial unsympathetic with Mormonism but insistent on 'the forty six-years of private citizenship on the part of David Whitmer, in Richmond, without stain or blemish.' " The very next year the newspaper's editor wrote a tribute to David on his eightieth birthday and noted the fact that David still "reiterates that he saw the glory of the angel." While few people in Richmond accepted the Book of Mormon and the miraculous vision beheld by David, "none doubted his intelligence or complete honesty."[14]

In another instance, an anti-Mormon published an encyclopedia article, claiming that David had denied his testimony. David printed a "proclamation," testifying to the truth of the Book of Mormon and reiterating the fact that he had never denied that testimony. He wrote:

> It is recorded in the American Cyclopedia and the Encyclopedia Britannica, that I, David Whitmer, have denied my testimony as one of the three witnesses to the divinity of the Book of Mormon; and that the two other witnesses, Oliver Cowdery and Martin Harris, denied their testimony to that book. I will say once more to all mankind, that I have never at any time denied that testimony or any part thereof. I also testify to the world, that neither Oliver Cowdery nor Martin Harris

ever at any time denied their testimony. They both died reaffirming the truth of the divine authenticity of the Book of Mormon.[15]

Attached to Whitmer's proclamation was an accompanying statement signed by twenty-two of Richmond's political, business, and professional leaders. They all certified that they had been "long and intimately acquainted" with Whitmer and knew him to be "a man of the highest integrity and of undoubted truth and veracity."[16]

A few days before Whitmer died, an article in the Chicago Tribune read: "David Whitmer, the last one of the three witnesses to the truth of the Book of Mormon, is now in a dying condition at his home in Richmond. Last evening he called the family and friends to his bedside, and bore his testimony to the truth of the Book of Mormon and the Bible."[17]

Following his death, the *Richmond Conservator* printed an article on the events preceding Whitmer's death. On the Sunday before his demise, he called his family and physician together and had the doctor concur that Whitmer was still in his right mind. Once he was satisfied that his family knew that he still retained his sanity, he said: "I want to give my dying testimony. You must be faithful in Christ. I want to say to you all that the Bible and the record of the Nephites, (The Book of Mormon) are true, so you can say that you have heard me bear my testimony on my death bed."[18]

The *Richmond Democrat* also added this comment: "Skeptics may laugh and scoff if they will, but no man can listen to Mr. Whitmer as he talks of his interview with the Angel of the Lord, without being most forcibly convinced that he has heard an honest man tell what he honestly believes to be true."[19]

Critics, of course, have argued that even if the Three Witnesses were honest, they could have experienced an episode of delusion or mass hypnosis. The visitation from an angel with plates, charge the critics, was all in their minds. David Whitmer—like the other witnesses—had been charged with being deluded into thinking he had seen an angel and the plates. One observer remembers when David was such accused, and how he responded: "How well and distinctly I remember the manner in which Elder Whitmer arose and drew himself up to his full height—a little over six feet—and said, in solemn and impressive tones: 'No sir! I was not under any hallucination, nor was I deceived! I saw with these eyes, and I heard with these ears! *I know whereof I speak!* "[20]

Marin Harris was also charged with being delusional and that he had merely imagined that he had seen an angel and the plates. Martin responded by extending his right hand and saying, "Gentlemen, do you see that hand? Are you sure you see it? Are your eyes playing you a trick or something? No. Well, as sure as you see my hand so sure did I see the angel and the plates."[21]

The testimony of the Eight Witnesses adds considerable support for the testimony of the Three Witnesses as well as the claims made by Joseph Smith. These eight men claimed to have handled physical metal plates—with the appearance of gold—that were engraved with odd characters. None of these men ever denied their testimonies despite the fact that many of them apostatized as well.

While the testimony of the Three Witnesses might be dismissed as hallucinatory, the same can not be logically argued for the Eight Witnesses. Either they were lying—which is unlikely given the fact that they all died true to their claims—or Joseph actually had golden plates. The combination of the Three and Eight Witnesses irritates all Mormon critics and presents a case that simply cannot be brushed aside. The testimony of the Eight provides a secular evidence that the testimony of the Three is real. It doesn't prove that the Three saw an angel, but it does provide strong evidence that Joseph really had golden plates. And if he had real golden plates, from where did he get them? How were they manufactured? Who engraved them? In what language were they written? So far, I have not seen any argument presented by a critic that successfully deals with the overwhelming evidence that Joseph had ancient golden plates.

As noted in section 4, Joseph wasn't wealthy enough to afford fake tin plates. Even if he had the financial means, however, the Eight Witnesses were tradesmen and farmers who worked with tin and other materials. They undoubtedly would have recognized a set of tin plates that were forged to look like an ancient golden record.

The very fact that eleven honest men testified to having seen or handled the golden plates is strong evidence for the truthfulness of the story as told by Joseph Smith.

6. Time of Translation

Both LDS and non-LDS historians generally agree that the time Joseph actually spent translating the Book of Mormon was very short. Joseph's first scribe, Martin Harris, ended up losing the first 116 pages of translated text. Joseph's wife, Emma, served as a scribe after Martin lost the position but very little was accomplished during this time because of the basic necessities of living. When Oliver Cowdery took over as scribe, the translation process charged full speed ahead.

By examining the timelines, scholars estimate that the entire Book of Mormon—over a quarter million words and nearly six hundred pages in the 1830 edition—was translated in a span of sixty-five to seventy-five days. That's an average of about seven to eight pages a day or over three thousand words a day. This means that 1 Nephi was likely translated in about one week and King Benjamin's discourse in about a day and a half. This is a miraculous achievement when we look at the complexity, depth, and profundity of what we find within the pages of this amazing book.[22]

7. Textual Consistency

More than a few LDS critics seem to think that it would be easy to produce a work like the Book of Mormon. One critic, for example, claims that the Book of Mormon is "exactly what one would expect from the pen of an imaginative but uneducated young man such as Joseph Smith."[23] Another critic wrote, "That a young man with a lively imagination, a smattering of the Bible, a passable ability at reading, an acquaintance with the theological debates of the day . . . could bring forth a book such as the *Book of Mormon* is not out of the question."[24]

Are the critics right? Would it be easy for an imaginative young man to produce a work like the Book of Mormon? If it's so easy, why hasn't any critic attempted to produce something like it? It's significant to note that the first critic is correct in that Joseph Smith was uneducated. Joseph was only about twenty-five when he translated the Nephite record; he had less than three years of formal schooling, may not have owned a Bible, and according to his mother, Joseph "had never read the Bible through in his life" and "seemed much less inclined to the perusal of books" than the rest of her children.[25] According to Emma, his wife, when Joseph first began translating, he could "neither write nor dictate a coherent and well worded letter; let alone . . . a book like the Book of Mormon."[26]

Not only does the book incorporate profound doctrinal insights, but it also discusses politics, war, geography, and migrations, and includes various sermons and a variety of specific events of distinct individuals. While estimating that Joseph produced about three thousand words of text a day, one critic pontificates, "Since this production did not involve the revision and rewriting by which authors usually polish their copy, the author/translator would be held back only by the ability of the secretary to take down the dictation."[27]

This point is a crucial piece of evidence in favor of the Book of Mormon—the original manuscript was not polished or revised by Joseph Smith. Emma, Joseph's wife, served as a scribe for part of the dictation. She recalled that when Joseph "stopped for any purpose at any time he would, when he commenced again, begin where he left off without any hesitation."[28] Emma and other witnesses also claim that Joseph had no notes, manuscripts, or books to which he would turn during the translation.[29] How does one keep a fictional story (or even an historical narrative) straight and consistent for nearly six hundred pages without forgetting at least some of the details of what had been written previously?

If the critics are correct, we should easily find many mistakes in chronology and the inter-connectivity of the many multiple events. Those who have actually studied the Book of Mormon find that it is a complex and an amazingly consistent text. "The Book of Mormon," wrote Dr. Hugh Nibley, "is a colossal structure. Considered purely a fiction, it is performance without parallel. What other volume can approach this wealth of detail and tight woven complexity, this factual precision combined with simple open lucidity? Any book we choose is feeble by comparison . . . this terse, compact religious history of a thousand years is something utterly beyond the scope of creative writing."[30]

Never once, notes Nibley, does the author of the Book of Mormon "get lost (as the student repeatedly does, picking his way out of one maze after another only with the greatest effort), and never once does he contradict himself. We should be glad to learn of any other like performance in the history of literature."[31] Following are a few examples of the amazing consistency we find in the Book of Mormon.

In Alma 36, Alma describes the joy he felt during his conversion and likens it to a scene from Lehi's vision wherein father Lehi "saw, God sitting upon his throne, surrounded with numberless concourses of angels, in the attitude of singing and praising their God" (Alma 36:22). These twenty-one words in Alma 36 are quoted verbatim from Nephi's record of Lehi's vision in 1 Nephi 1:8 (which is 319 pages earlier in the first edition of the Book of Mormon). How many readers of this book could quote twenty-one words from the previous page without looking?

In 1 Nephi 19:11–12, Nephi records the prophecy of the ancient prophet Zenos concerning the destruction that would come upon the wicked. Zenos lists ten calamities including lightning, fire, vapor of darkness, and more. These same ten calamities are shown to have occurred in 3 Nephi 8:6–23 (four hundred and twenty pages later in the original edition), preceding the visitation of Christ.

Last, in Mosiah 2:13 King Benjamin lists five legal prohibitions: murder, plunder, theft, adultery, and any manner of wickedness. These same exact five prohibitions are found seven other times in the Book of Mormon as part of Nephite formulaic law.[32]

8. Evidence for Dictation

In contrast to some popular artwork we see in the Church, the historical record indicates that Joseph Smith translated the Book of Mormon by putting the Nephite Interpreters (Mormon 9:34 and Ether 4:5) or his seer stone into an upside-down hat. He then put his face in the hat to shield all ambient light and by the power of God would see an English translation of the Book of Mormon characters which he dictated to a scribe.

Although the method of translation has been mentioned in Church literature such as the *Ensign* magazine, some members seem shocked when they find that their perceptions about the translation mechanics employed by Joseph don't conform to what they previously envisioned. Some members are surprised because they had been taught that Joseph translated the plates by way of the Urim and Thummim. This is true. What most members don't realize, however, is that Urim and Thummim was the name given both to the Nephite Interpreters that were included in the stone box with the plates, as well as a seer stone that Joseph owned and later used to receive revelations.

How, some have asked, could Joseph receive revelation through a seer stone in a hat? This is an odd question for a believing member. Are we to understand that translating the plates with a rock outside of a hat (the Nephite "interpreters") is preferable to translating with a rock inside a hat (the seer stone)? If Joseph Smith was a prophet, and if the translation came by the gift and power of God, does the method of translation matter?

Joseph never revealed the details of the translation process, but he and other witnesses left enough clues that we are able to surmise some of the things that likely transpired. Most members think (and unfortunately this is supported by some LDS art) that Joseph Smith sat at a table with the plates dictating while a scribe sat on the other side of a curtain recording Joseph's words.

During the early part of dictation process with Martin Harris, there was, indeed, a curtain stretched between Martin and Joseph. It's possible that the curtain was used only once—when Joseph copied some of the plate's characters for Martin to take to have examined by Professor Anthon. The majority of the translating was done in plain sight of the scribe and others while the plates themselves were covered or hidden. As one interviewer learned from David Whitmer, a blanket was stretched between the Whitmer's living room and the rest of the house, so Joseph and his scribes could translate without being disturbed by visitors. According to Whitmer, the blanket was not used to conceal the plates or translators from the scribes. In fact, noted Whitmer, Joseph performed the translation in the presence of the "entire Whitmer household and several of Smith's relatives."[33]

We also know that the process was not completely automatic—Joseph had to apply some thought to the words that appeared before him. When Oliver Cowdery made a failed attempt to translate, for instance, God told Oliver: "Behold, you have not understood; you have supposed that I would give it unto you, when you took no thought save it was to ask me. But, behold, I say unto you, that you must study it out in your mind; then you must ask me if it be right, and if it is right I will cause that your bosom shall burn within you; therefore, you shall feel that it is right" (D&C 9:7–8).

With the exception of names (which will be discussed later), it seems that Joseph may have seen or felt concepts that he had to formulate into English sentences. Early LDS Apostle Orson Pratt explained, Joseph "received the *ideas* from God, but clothed those *ideas* with such *words* as came to his mind."[34]

Those concepts may have come as very literal translations from what was on the plates, but Joseph would have had to restructure the translation into something more intelligible in English. At times (see section 13) Joseph may have followed the literal translations too closely.

Second, we know that when Joseph encountered unfamiliar proper nouns, he would spell them out the first time. Initially, for example, Oliver Cowdery wrote "Coriantummer" after which he crossed it out and wrote "Coriantumr" above the crossed-out word. Oliver could not have known that Coriantumr was spelled "tumr" unless he was corrected in his spelling by Joseph Smith during the dictation.

Third, we find strong evidence for dictation from a study of the original manuscript itself. Dr. Royal Skousen, an internationally recognized linguist theorist, has spent several decades studying the original Book of Mormon manuscript as penned by Joseph's scribes and has discovered numerous clues—typically in the form of scribal errors—that indicate the text was written from dictation. I'll share three examples.

Sometimes the scribe heard and wrote *and* for what should have been *an*. In the original manuscript, 1 Nephi 13:29 reads:

> & because of these things which are taken out of the gosple [sic] of the lamb & exceeding great many do stumble

The second ampersand (&)—denoting *and*—should be *an* but the scribe, writing fast enough to keep up with Joseph's dictation, heard "and" and therefore used an ampersand.

In another instance Oliver Cowdery misheard Joseph as he dictated Alma 57:22. In the original manuscript he wrote: "for it was they who did meet the Lamanites." The word *meet* is crossed out and the word *beat* is inserted above it. This is not the kind of mistake that one makes when reading or copying a document, but it is the precise kind of mistake someone makes when they mishear what is dictated. Third, in at least two instances, Oliver heard Joseph say "'em" and wrote "him" but immediately corrected the word to "them."[35]

Skousen also finds evidence that Joseph must have seen twenty to thirty words at a time which he dictated to the scribes in blocks. Some scribal errors, for instance, indicate that sometimes the scribe would get ahead of himself in the dictating process. For example, in Alma 56:41, the scribe wrote:

> & it came to pass that again [we saw the Lamanites]
> when the light of the morning came we saw the Lamanites upon us

In the scripture above, the bracketed "we saw the Lamanites" is crossed out. Apparently, Joseph dictated this twenty-word block and the scribe—trying to keep up—wrote "we saw the Lamanites" too soon, accidently skipping "when the light of the morning came." When he realized that he had skipped that part of the dictation, he crossed it out, and correctly finished this twenty-word section.

Another example comes from Alma 45:22 where we find the earliest extant example of Joseph Smith's own handwriting. In the middle of dictation, Oliver takes a sudden break, and Joseph finishes off a twenty-eight word block in his own handwriting. Joseph may have already seen the block of text in his translators and took the opportunity to write down the remaining portion while waiting for Oliver to return. A clue to the necessity of writing down what Joseph saw—while it was still in view—might be found in a statement of Joseph Smith's wife, Emma: "I am satisfied that no man could have dictated the writing of the manuscripts unless he was inspired; for, when acting as his scribe, your father would dictate to me hour after hour; and when returning after meals, or after interruptions, he would at once begin where he had left off, without either seeing the manuscript or having any portion of it read to him."[36]

It's possible that Joseph had to engage what he saw in the interpreters while they were still visible, otherwise the information would disappear from view and move on to the next block of text.

Since Joseph's face was buried in a hat—which excluded all light—he couldn't have been reading from scraps of paper, and as noted above, Joseph didn't have any books or manuscripts at hand during the translation process. That Joseph dictated this complex manuscript, at blocks of twenty to thirty words at a time, and never went back to review earlier portions of the manuscript, is a remarkable feat that has never been reproduced by any critic.

9. Book of Mormon Politics Unlike Joseph Smith's

In 1976, during America's bicentennial, LDS historian Richard Bushman was preparing a speech and turned to the Book of Mormon to find some quotes that would resonate with the principals in our Constitution. To his surprise, he found that—besides some superficial similarities—the Book of Mormon did not reflect typical US political thought. Instead, Bushman found that the Nephite scripture was "an anomaly on the political scene of 1830." He continues, "Instead of heroically resisting despots, the people of God fled their oppressors and credited God alone with deliverance. Instead of enlightened people overthrowing their kings in defense of their natural rights, the common people repeatedly raised up kings, and the prophets and the kings themselves had to persuade the people of the inexpediency of monarchy."[37]

According to Bushman, the Book of Mormon is "strangely distant from the time and place of its publication" but its political attitudes are at home when we compare it to the history of the Israelites.[38]

Joseph Smith lived in an era that idolized many of the heroes from the Revolutionary War. Some of Joseph's own ancestors had fought in that war. Joseph's own words and actions show that his personal philosophies were like those of his patriotic contemporaries. Critics have often argued that Joseph wrote the Book of Mormon simply by sponging the information from his environment and attempting to answer the concerns of his day. The Book of Mormon, however, doesn't engage "the most common American attitudes toward a revolution, monarchy, and the limitations of power" that we find in the political landscape of Joseph's milieu.

In the Nephite record, we find that elections are rare, there is no written constitution, and there is no separation of powers. "The Book of Mormon is not a conventional American book," argues Bushman. Instead, the book should be understood according to the "ancient patterns" deeply ingrained in the Nephite narrative.[39]

NOTES

1. Reprinted in *Early Mormon Documents,* 5 vols., ed. Dan Vogel (Salt Lake City, UT: Signature Books, 1996), 1:511.
2. Ibid., 1:505.
3. Ibid., 1:221.
4. Ibid., 1:541.
5. Ibid., 1:524–25.
6. Interview with Martin Harris, "Mormonism," *Tiffany's Monthly,* August 1859, 169.
7. Quoted in William J. Hamblin, "An Apologist for the Critics: Brent Lee Metcalfe's Assumptions and Methodologies," *Review of Books on the Book of Mormon* (1994) 6:1, 515.
8. *Lucy Mack Smith,* 111.
9. Reprinted in *Early Mormon Documents,* 1:511, 512.
10. Ibid., 1:496.
11. Quoted in "Book of Mormon Witnesses/Recant" on FAIRwiki at http://en.fairmormon.org/Book_of_Mormon_witnesses/Recant#ref_cowdery3 (accessed 4 July 2008).
12. Quoted in William E. Berrett, *The Restored Church* (Salt Lake City: Deseret Book, 1977), 57–58.
13. Quoted in Michael R. Ash, "Book of Mormon Witnesses, Part 3: Martin Harris," at http://www.fairlds.org/FAIR_Brochures/Book_of_Mormon_Witnesses_3.pdf (accessed 4 July 2008).
14. Richard L. Anderson, *Investigating the Book of Mormon Witnesses* (Salt Lake City, UT: Deseret Book, 1981), 74.
15. David Whitmer, *An Address to All Believers in Christ* (Richmond, Missouri, 1887), 8.
16. Richard L. Anderson, *Investigating the Book of Mormon Witness,* 74-75
17. Reprinted in *David Whitmer Interviews: A Restoration Witness,* ed., Lyndon W. Cook (Orem, UT: Grandin Book Co., 1991), 220.
18. Ibid., 226.
19. Quoted in Michael R. Ash, "Book of Mormon Witnesses, Part 4:

David Whitmer," at http://www.fairlds.org/FAIR_Brochures/Book_ of_Mormon_Witnesses_4.pdf (accessed 4 July 2008).

20. Quoted in Anderson, *Investigating the Book of Mormon Witnesses*, 88.

21. Ibid., 116.

22. "How Long Did It Take to Translate the Book of Mormon?" *Reexploring the Book of Mormon,* ed. John W. Welch (Salt Lake City, UT: Deseret Book, 1992), 1–4.

23. Decker and Hunt, *The God Makers,* 111.

24. Whalen, *The Latter-day Saints in the Modern Day World,* 40.

25. Reprinted in *Early Mormon Documents,* 1:296.

26. Ibid., 1:539.

27. Whalen, *The Latter-day Saints in the Modern Day World,* 40.

28. Reprinted in *Early Mormon Documents,* 1:530.

29. Ibid., 539.

30. Hugh Nibley, *Since Cumorah* (Salt Lake City, UT: Deseret Book, 1967), 156–57.

31. Hugh Nibley, "The Book of Mormon: True or False?" *The Prophetic Book of Mormon* (Salt Lake City, UT: Deseret Book; Provo: FARMS, 1989), 225.

32. These examples are found in "Textual Consistency," *Reexploring the Book of Mormon,* 21–23.

33. Daniel C. Peterson, "Not So Easily Dismissed," *The FARMS Review* 17, no. 2 (2005): xvii.

34. Quoted by Robert J. Woodford, "The Story of the Doctrine & Covenants," *Ensign,* Dec. 1984, 34.

35. Royal Skousen, "Translating the Book of Mormon: Evidence from the Original Manuscript," *Book of Mormon Authorship Revisited: The Evidence for Ancient Origins,* ed. Noel B. Reynolds (Provo, UT: FARMS, 1997), 68.

36. Reprinted in *Early Mormon Documents,* 1:542.

37. Richard L. Bushman, "The Book of Mormon and the American Revolution," *Believing History: Latter-day Saint Essays* (New York: Columbia University Press, 2004), 57.

38. Ibid.

39. Ibid., 59.

Book of Mormon Language

10. Word Prints

Because critics are determined to find any source for the Book of Mormon other than the one presented by believers, they generally claim that Joseph either wrote the book himself or that he plagiarized the text from some other nineteenth-century author. As a critic in 1838 charged: "The sameness of the language in all parts of the book [sic] of Mormon proves that it is from the same hand."[1] The invention of the computer has brought a new tool with which to test a document's authorship. Wordprint studies (or stylometry) can detect an author's fingerprint style by the individual word patterns they use for non-contextual words such as *a, of, the,* and *it.* These patterns are typically unconscious to the author and are not easily altered.[2]

Stylometry was first proposed in 1851 (twenty-one years after the Book of Mormon was published), but it wasn't until the invention of the computer before stylometric tests could be done with a high degree of accuracy. There are at least two well-known cases in which non-Mormon researchers were able to determine authorship thanks to Stylometry. The first concerns the authorship of twelve of the eighty-five Federalist Papers. Scholars have long debated whether Alexander Hamilton or James Madison wrote those twelve papers. Using word prints, scholars from Harvard and the University of Chicago determined that Madison had authored all twelve papers.

Our second example involves an anonymous author who completed an unfinished novel of Jane Austin's after she died in 1817. This anonymous author was able to fool the public with a style that imitated Jane Austin but her unconscious elements of style were unable to fool the computer when a word print was performed.[3]

Using the same methods, other scholars have compared the personal writings of Joseph Smith, Oliver Cowdery, and other contemporaries, to the authors in the Book of Mormon. The outcome? According to the experts who conducted the research, word prints conclusively demonstrate that the Book of Mormon was written by many authors (there were twenty-four distinct word prints)—none of which matched Joseph Smith or the contemporaries tested.[4]

Newer updated studies, designed to assure greater accuracy, have reached the same conclusion. While the work is obviously not definitive, as it currently stands, the Book of Mormon word prints are uniquely different from the word prints of Joseph Smith, Oliver Cowdery, as well as other contemporaries who have been suggested to be the real source for the Book of Mormon.[5]

11. Chiasmus

While on a mission in Germany in 1967, John Welch attended a Catholic-taught class on the New Testament. In this class Welch discovered that New Testament scholars had recently become aware of an ancient Hebrew literary form called chiasmus. The word is Greek, deriving from the twenty-second letter of the Greek alphabet, chi (X), and the Greek *chiazein,* meaning to mark with a X. Thus a chiasmus takes the form of an X—to cross over. A chiastic passage is arranged so that the first and last elements parallel each other, the second and second to last elements parallel each other, and so forth into the center. The apex—or center of the chiasmus—is the central point of the passage. This literary form was virtually unknown in the western world during Joseph Smith's day.

After some additional research, Welch wondered if chiasmus could be found in the Book of Mormon since it claimed a Near Eastern background. As Welch's investigation progressed, he found that not only did the Book of Mormon contain chiastic structures, but some of these structures were very elaborate and complex. Following is just a small sampling of the many complex chiasmus found in the Book of Mormon.

And now whosoever shall not take upon them the *name of Christ*
must be *called* by some other name;
  therefore he findeth himself on the *left hand of God.*
   And I would that ye should *remember* that this is the name
    that should never be *blotted out*
     except it be through *transgression:*
     therefore
     take heed that ye do not *transgress*
    that the name be not *blotted* out of your hearts.
   I would that ye should *remember* to retain this name
  that ye are not found on the *left hand of God,*
but that ye hear and know the voice by which ye shall be *called*
and also the *name* by which he shall call you. (Mosiah 5:10–12)[6]

[Overview of Helaman 6:7–13:]
A "And behold, there was *peace* in all the land" (6:7).
 B Freedom of travel and trade in *both lands* is discussed (6:7–8).
  C "And it came to pass that they became exceeding *rich,* both the Lamanites and Nephites;
   D and they did have an exceeding *plenty* of *gold,* and of *silver,* and of *all manner* of *precious metals, both* in the *land* south and in the *land* north" (6:9).
    E "Now the land *south*
    was called *Lehi* and
    the land *north*
    was called *Mulek*
    which was after the son of Zedek*iah*;
    for the *Lord* [in Hebrew, the Godly suffix is *yah*]
    did bring *Mulek*
    into the land *north*
    and *Lehi*
    into the land *south"* (6:10).
   D "And behold there was *all manner* of *gold* in *both* these *lands* and of *silver* and of *precious ore* of *every kind;*
  C and there were also curious workmen, who did work all kinds of ore and did refine it; and thus they did become *rich"* (6:11).
 B Economic prosperity in *both lands* is discussed (6:12–13).
A "And thus the sixty and fourth year did pass away in *peace"* (6:13).[7]

Adding to the remarkable nature of this particular chiasmus is the fact that at the center, or apex, are the parallel words *Zedekiah* and *Lord*. The Hebrew word for *Lord* is equivalent to the suffix "yah" which we find (with a variant spelling) at the end of the name *Zedekiah*.

It is important to emphasize once again that for all intents, chiasmus was unknown in the United States when the Book of Mormon was published. And even if Joseph had some sort of scholarly knowledge unavailable to the typical frontiersman, how did he find time—during the seventy or so days of translating—to create such complex chiastic structures? The presence of chiasmus in the Book of Mormon lends support to the claim that the book is based on an authentic ancient text.

12. If/And Conditional Sentences

Dr. Daniel Peterson and Dr. Royal Skousen recently discovered that the Book of Mormon contains odd sentence structures utilizing the conditions *if* and *and*. In the original Book of Mormon manuscript, as dictated by Joseph to Oliver Cowdery, we find several examples such as the following:

> . . . yea and *if* he saith unto the earth move *and* it is moved . . .

> . . . yea *if* he say unto the earth thou shalt go back that it lengthen out the day for many hours *and* it is done . . .

> . . . and behold also *if* he saith unto the waters of the great deep be thou dried up *and* it is done . . .

In modern editions of the Book of Mormon, these phrases were edited to sound more grammatically correct to English readers.

The "if/and" conditional sentence structure is found in the original Book of Mormon manuscript as well as in ancient Hebrew and biblical Hebrew. Like modern editions of the Book of Mormon, however, the King James Version of the Bible was modified to make it more palatable to English readers by removing the "if/and" sentences. As far as the research of Skousen and Peterson have shown, this authentic Hebrew sentence structure was not available in any other English text in Joseph Smith's lifetime but is a strong evidence for the Hebraic background of the Book of Mormon text.[8]

13. Hebraisms

Like the "if/and" conditional sentence structure above, we now know that many of the Book of Mormon expressions which are ungrammatical in English (especially in the first edition) are perfectly grammatical in Hebrew. It's important to note that it was a full five years after the Book of Mormon was translated before Joseph began to study Hebrew, and it was decades later before the first LDS scholars noticed the many Hebraisms in Joseph's translation.

If Joseph might have known Hebrew before translating the Book of Mormon, why didn't he or any of the LDS scholars of his lifetime point out the Hebrew grammar structure in the Book of Mormon? Not only did the Mormons not notice the Hebrew structure, but neither did the critics. Some of Joseph's loudest critics were the learned ministers. One would think that at least one of those ministers, with their theological and seminary training, would have mentioned the Hebraisms or Mormon claims of Hebraisms if it would have been noticed in the early days of the Church. The fact is that no one noticed these Hebrew idioms until much later.

One of the standard charges against the Book of Mormon has been its poor grammar. Critics have claimed that this is evidence that Joseph wrote—as opposed to translated—the book, while Mormons have claimed that the poor grammar is indicative of Joseph utilizing his own language when translating into English.

Although the Book of Mormon language had undergone nearly a thousand years of change by the time Mormon compiled and edited the text, it's possible that enough of the Hebrew language survived that idioms can be found throughout the book—most noticeably in the first and earliest portion of the work. 1 Nephi through Omni (which were written on what Book of Mormon prophets called the "Small Plates") were written not long after the Lehites fled Jerusalem and therefore had the best chance of retaining Hebrew idioms. As we examine the text, we find that such is the case.

For example, in Hebrew and on the Small Plates, a man does not "marry a woman," but he "takes her to wife." Therefore we read in 1 Nephi 7:1 that "his sons should take daughters to wife." In Hebrew, *and* is used before each word in a series or list. We find the same thing in the Small Plates such as in "because of their iniquities, *and* the hardness of their hearts, *and* the stiffness of their necks" (2 Nephi 25:12; italics added).

In Enos 1:21 we read: "And it came to pass that the people of Nephi did till the land, *and* raise all manner of grain, *and* of fruit, *and* flocks of herds, *and* flocks of all manner of cattle of every kind, *and* goats, *and* wild goats, *and* also many horses" (italics added).

In Hebrew, if several nouns are coupled by a conjunction, the possessive pronoun must be repeated with each noun. In the Small Plates we read: "with *our* bows and *our* arrows and *our* stones and *our* slings" (1 Nephi 16:15; italics added). We find the same thing with prepositions, as in "wherefore I did arm myself *with* a bow and a arrow, *with* a sling and *with* stones" (1 Nephi 16:23; italics added). We also have the following examples:

> And he left *his* house, and the land of *his* inheritance, and *his* gold, and *his* silver, and *his* precious things. (1 Nephi 1:29; italics added.)

> To leave the land of *their* inheritance, and *their* gold, and *their* silver, and *their* precious things. (1 Nephi 1:38; italics added.)

> *Our* gold, and *our* silver, and all *our* precious things. (1 Nephi 1:87; italics added.)[9]

While it might be tempting to think that particles such as "and with" and "and their" would waste precious space on the Book of Mormon plates, they are necessary items in both Hebrew and Egyptian and they actually take up very little space compared to their English counterparts.[10]

Another Hebraism uncommon in English is the "construct state." In the Book of Mormon, for instance, we read of an "altar of stones" (1 Nephi 2:7) instead of "stone altar"; "plates of brass" (1 Nephi 3:3) and never "brass plates"; "words of plainness" (Jacob 4:14) rather than "plain words"; "skin of blackness" (2 Nephi 5:21) instead of "black skin"; "vapor of darkness" (1 Nephi 12:5) instead of "dark vapor"; "rod of iron" (1 Nephi 8:19) and never "iron rod"; "daughters of Ishmael"; "house of Laban"; and the list goes on and on.

In Hebrew, prepositions are commonly used to produce adverbs such as the Book of Mormon's "with harshness" (instead of "harshly"), "with joy" (instead of "joyfully"), "with gladness," "with patience," "with diligence," "in diligence," "in abundance," "of worth," and others.

In subsequent printings of the Book of Mormon, several instances of "that" and "which" were changed to "who" and "whom"—this was necessary for proper English. In Hebrew, however, the relative pronoun *aser* translates as either "that" or "which" as well as "who" or "whom."[11]

Dr. David P. Wright, a non-LDS Near Eastern scholar from Brandeis University, does not believe in the antiquity of the Book of Mormon, but nevertheless notes that the research published by FARMS and other LDS scholars "has shown on occasion some striking coincidences between elements in the Book of Mormon and the ancient world and some notable matters of Book of Mormon style."[12]

Dr. Sidney Sperry. who spent many years studying the Hebraisms in the Book of Mormon, claimed that a "far stronger case can be made" that the Book of Mormon was translated closely from an original Hebrew text, "than can be made for the Four Gospels as translation Greek as seen in the work of certain scholars . . . of Yale University."[13] According to Sperry, "the Book of Mormon often betrays a too literal adherence to an apparent Hebrew original."[14]

14. The "Rent" Garment, Part 1

In Alma 46 we read that Captain Moroni made a "banner of liberty" from his rent coat. In the original edition of the Book of Mormon on page 351 we read: "And when Moroni had said these words, he went forth among the people, waving the rent of his garment in the air, that all might see the writing which he had *wrote upon the rent,* and crying with a loud voice. . . ." (italics added).

For clarification and to improve the grammar, the current edition of the Book of Mormon reads: "And when Moroni had said these words, he went forth among the people, waving the rent part of his garment in the air, that all might see the writing which he had *written upon the rent part,* and crying with a loud voice. . . ." (Alma 46:19; italics added).

Critics have laughed at the original version for more than a century. To them, this was one more proof that the unsophisticated Joseph Smith wrote—rather than translated—the Book of Mormon. How can a "rent" be written upon?

In Hebrew the word *qera'*—which is translated as a noun for a "rent part"—derives from the Hebrew *qara'* which is the verb form and means "he rent, tore." This word also translates in a manner that makes "rent" a noun—just as we find in Alma 46.[15] The charge of the critics has backfired.

15. "It Came to Pass," Part 1

The Book of Mormon's frequent use of the phrase "and it came to pass" has been the target of much ridicule. Mark Twain claimed this was Smith's most frequently used "pet" phrase. Had Smith left it out, teased Twain, the Book of Mormon "would have been only a pamphlet."[16] The charge has been repeated by various anti-Mormons, including one critic who, in 1979, claimed that the Book of Mormon "is cursed with the clumsy, repetitious phrase 'and it came to pass' that appears hundreds of times in the book, on almost every page."[17] Neither Mark Twain nor Joseph Smith would have known in the nineteenth century just how important the phrase was to Book of Mormon authors.

The original manuscript of the Book of Mormon had no punctuation. Likewise, manuscripts prior to the tenth century typically had no punctuation. In both ancient Egyptian and Hebrew indicator phrases, such as "it came to pass," "and now," "and thus," and similar monotonous phrases, were grammatically necessary to denote new thoughts or paragraphs.[18] Since the Book of Mormon claims to be written in a modified Hebrew language and "reformed" or modified Egyptian characters, it would be strange if *didn't* contain such phrases.

16. "Reformed Egyptian"

Near the beginning of the Book of Mormon, Nephi tells his readers that the record was written in "the language of my father, which consists of the learning of the Jews and the language of the Egyptians" (1 Nephi 1:2). Near the end of the book (about one thousand years later) the Nephite prophet Moroni tells us that the record was written "in the characters which are called among us the reformed Egyptian, being handed down and altered by us, according to our manner of speech" (Mormon 9:33–34). Moroni goes on to explain that they would have liked to have written in Hebrew, but reformed Egyptian took up less space on the plates. He also recognizes that over the intervening thousand years, their Hebrew had been altered and would be different from the Hebrew of Lehi's day. Realizing that no one but the Lord and a handful of Nephites knew this unique script, he trusted the Lord to prepare a means that the text could be interpreted.

First, the critics have assured us for years that devout Israelites such as Lehi would not have written scripture in a pagan Egyptian script but would *only* have used Hebrew. "Let any Mormonite produce a specimen of such a language if he can," chided one critic in 1838.[19]

Second, they assure us that there is no such thing as reformed Egyptian. Nearly fifty years ago, however, Hugh Nibley showed that the Egyptian culture played an influential role in seventh century BC Palestine—primarily in the area of culture and language. Modern studies verify that Nibley was right. Recently rediscovered writings from approximately Lehi's day tell us that Jews and other foreigners were all instructed in the language of Egypt. We now know of other Hebrew and Aramaic texts—such as *Papyrus Amherst 63*—that were written in Egyptian characters. For many years, Egyptologists were unable to decipher the documents until they realized that the underlying texts were not Egyptian. Just over a decade ago, for instance, it was discovered that some ancient potsherds from Lehi's vicinity and time contained a script composed of a modified form of Egyptian hieroglyphics. This script was used almost exclusively by Israel and not any of the neighboring communities. Some Near Eastern scholars now believe that scribes and students in Lehi's day were trained in both Hebrew and Egyptian writings systems.

The claim that there is no such thing as reformed Egyptian is a hollow argument. *Reformed* is an adjective—not a noun—and is synonymous with *altered*, or *modified*. Today's scholars use terms such as *cuneiform*, and *hieroglyphics*. These are modern non-Egyptian terms given to scripts by modern scholars. The ancient Egyptians used three different types of writing systems. *Hieroglyphs* (Greek for "sacred symbols") used nearly four hundred picture characters that depicted things from real life. *Hieratic* (Greek for "sacred") was a cursive script used primarily on papyrus. *Demotic* (Greek for "popular") was an even more cursive script. These latter two were used during Lehi's day and can properly be called "reformed Egyptian."[20]

There are currently enough historical examples of modified or reformed Egyptian texts to validate the Book of Mormon's claim to the same phenomenon.

17. The Name "Nephi"

Critics typically contend that Joseph either invented the names in the Book of Mormon or borrowed them from his surroundings. The first name mentioned in the Nephite record is *Nephi*. We find this name in the Apocrypha. The Apocrypha are part of the Catholic collection of scriptures (which was available in Joseph's day) but is not included in the Protestant scriptures such as the King James Version Bible. Whether Joseph had access to the Apocrypha in 1829 is unknown.

If we look to see if the name *Nephi* is at home in the world of Lehi, we find confirmation. In the vicinity and time in which the Lehites lived in the Old World, we have attestations of names that could be translated into English as *Nephi*. We don't know how Book of Mormon names were pronounced, but typical readers have given the *i* in Nephi a long sound, whereas a long *e* sound is equally plausible.

From ancient Egypt during Lehi's day, we find the name Nfr. By the time the Lehites fled Jerusalem in the fifth century BC, the *r* in Nfr was no longer pronounced and a long *e* sound had taken its place.[21] While not a direct hit, it does show that the name is at home in the right place and at the right time as the Book of Mormon claims.

18. The Name "Sariah"

Sariah was Lehi's faithful wife who endured so much tribulation during their journey through the Arabian Peninsula. Dr. Jeffrey Chadwick, who holds a PhD in Archaeology and Semitic Languages, believes that a likely "Hebrew spelling of *Sariah* would be *s'ryh* and would be pronounced something like *Sar-yah*." It is interesting therefore to note that the name *s'ryh* has been found on some ancient Aramaic papyri in Egypt, dating to the time of Lehi, that was not discovered until the twentieth century. Although the language of the document is Aramaic, the name, it has been shown, is Hebrew. Non-Mormon scholars have translated this part of the papyri as "Sariah daughter of Hoshea son of Harman." While variations of *s'ryh* have been previously known for males, this was the first time that the name has been shown to belong to women in the same general area and time as what we find in the Book of Mormon.[22]

19. The Names "Paanchi" and "Pahoran"

In Helaman chapter 1 we read of Paanchi, one of the sons of Pahoran who fought with his brothers for the judgment seat following their father's death. While the names may sound made-up to some, we now know that they are authentic Egyptian names and were unlikely to have been available to Joseph Smith.

Scholars at the Maxwell Institute relate the story of William F. Albright—a renowned (non-LDS) Near Eastern scholar at John Hopkins University—who responded to a critic eliciting negative comments about LDS scriptures. Albright said he was surprised to find Paanchi and Pahoran—two authentic Egyptian names—in the Book of Mormon. He also noted that the names appear in close reference to the original Book of Mormon language being written in reformed Egyptian. He didn't know how to explain the appearance of these names and doubted that Joseph could have learned Egyptian from any early nineteenth century source. Perhaps, Albright suggested, Joseph Smith was some kind of "religious genius."[23]

20. Alma as a Male Name

Many critics have laughed at the Book of Mormon for using "Alma" as a masculine personal name. In the United States, Alma is typically a female name of Latin origin. Alma-mater, for example, means "nourishing mother" and was used during medieval times to refer to the Virgin Mary.

In the late twentieth-century, however, it was found that some ancient Near Eastern documents—such as letters from Bar Kokhba and clay tablets from Ebla—contained the male name "Alma." The Book of Mormon correctly uses the name for the right gender in the correct language family, and in the correct part of the ancient Old World.[24]

21. Mulek, Son of Zedekiah

In Omni Chapter 1 we read that the Lord warned Mosiah that the Lamanites were about to attack the land of Nephi. Mosiah was told to flee and to take all who would listen with him. During their flight they discovered the people of Zarahemla whose descendants had also lived in Jerusalem under the reign of Zedekiah. In 586 BC Babylonian troops under King Nebuchadrezzar breached the walls of Jerusalem and destroyed the city. Mulek, one of the sons of Zedekiah, escaped the Babylonians, fled Jerusalem, landed in the New World, and helped found the people of Zarahemla.

According to the Bible, King Nebuchadrezzar "slew the sons of Zedekiah before his eyes," slew "all the princes of Judah in Riblah," then "put out the eyes of Zedekiah," "bound him in chains," and carried him captive to Babylon where he died in prison (Jeremiah 52:10–11). Verse 10 has led most Bible students to believe that all of Zedekiah's sons were killed by the Babylonians. The Book of Mormon, however, tells us that Mulek was a surviving son of Zedekiah (Helaman 8:21). Modern scholarship suggests that the Book of Mormon is right.

Yohanan Aharoni, the late (non-LDS) head of the Department of Archaeology at Tel Aviv University, claims that one of the contemporary sons of King Zedekiah was named Malkiyahu. This is supported by the recent discovery of a seal engraved with "MalkiYahu, son of the King."

But how could Malkiyahu be Mulek? It was a common ancient practice to shorten some names. Jeremiah, for instance, shortened his scribe's name BerekYahu to Baruch. Ancient Hebrew had no vowels and *Mulek* would carry the proper root consonants for an abbreviated form of Malkiyahu (in both cases the names are shortened by the removal of "yahu"). According to the researchers who have examined this issue, one prominent non-LDS ancient Near Eastern specialist was in general agreement that "MalkiYahu, son of the King," could be a son of King Zedekiah and that a short-form of the name could be Mulek. The vowels in *Mulek,* he explained, could be a Phoenician pronunciation. When he was shown that the Book of Mormon listed "Mulek" as one of Zedekiah's sons he declared: "If Joseph Smith came up with that one, he did pretty good!"[25]

22. Deseret and Bees

In Ether 2:3 we find that the Jaredite word *deseret* means "honeybee." Years ago, Dr. Nibley observed that the word *deseret* "or something very close to it, enjoyed a position of ritual prominence" among the early Egyptians and they associated the word with a symbol of the bee. He explained, "We know that the bee sign was not always written down, but in its place the picture of the Red Crown . . . If we do not know the original name of the bee, we do know the name of this Red Crown—the name it bore when it was substituted for the bee. The name was *dsrt* (the vowels are not known, but we can be sure they were all short)."[26]

23. More Names

With the exception of Alma, Book of Mormon names have not usually received much attention from detractors. The few times that the critics have mentioned Book of Mormon names has been, in typical anti-Mormon style, to ridicule them as strange and obviously created by Joseph Smith. One such learned critic wrote: "It required something of a genius, it must be confessed, to manufacture some of the *names* of the Book of Mormon . . . names that at least have a certain syllabic jingle, if they have no meaning."[27]

As light is shed on all areas of Book of Mormon studies, however, we gain new support for the names found in the Nephite scripture. Many Book of Mormon names, we find, have Near Eastern parallels, several of which are Egyptian. "It should be noted," writes Nibley, "that archaeology has fully demonstrated that the Israelites, then as now, had not the slightest aversion to giving their children non-Jewish names, even when those names smacked of a pagan background."[28] Recently discovered ancient manuscripts show that many Jews, in the days of Lehi, named their children after Egyptian hero kings of the past.[29]

Nibley has done extensive research into the comparison of Book of Mormon names with authentic ancient Old World names—below are some of his comparisons. First we list just a sampling of Book of Mormon names, followed by their Old World equivalents:

Aha = Aha

Ammon = Ammon;

Hem = Hem;

Helaman = Her-amon (as Nibley notes, "the "Semitic 'l' is always written 'r' in Egyptian, which has no 'l.' Conversely, the Egyptian 'r' is often written 'l' in Semitic languages"[30]);

Korihor = Kherihor;

Manti = Manti;

Pachus = Pa-ks or Pach-qs

Zenoch = Zenekh.[31]

Nibley points out that for some reason, the Book of Mormon does not include a single name containing the element of Baal, which is so common in the Old Testament. This had confused Mormon scholars until the recent discovery of the Elephantine papyrus from Egypt. The names in these manuscripts show that the Israelites eliminated all names with *Baal* elements during Lehi's day. Of the over four hundred names among the Elephantine manuscripts, not one is compounded of *Baal*.[32] In addition, Nibley explains that a "large proportion of Book of Mormon names end in *-iah* and *-ihah*. The same ending is peculiar to Palestinian names of Lehi's time but not of other times."[33]

The name *Lehi* is an interesting example of Joseph Smith's prophetic abilities. In the Bible it occurs only as part of a place name. Not long ago, however, the name *LHI-TN*, son of Pagag, whose names means, "Lehi hath given," was found inscribed on some stones in Arabia.[34] We also find that the names of Lehi's eldest sons, Laman and Lemuel, "are not only 'Arabic' names but they also form a genuine 'pair of pendant names,' such as ancient Semites of the desert were wont to give their two eldest sons."[35]

After leaving their base camp, the first important place the Lehites stopped was at a place called Shazer (1 Nephi 16:13–14). In Palestine the word *shajer*, often pronounced shazher, means "trees." Sometimes the word is confused with the Palestinian *Shaghur,* which means "seepage," usually referring to a weak, albeit reliable, water supply. One now-famous South Arabian water hole has been labeled in various forms of the word—Sozura, Shisur, and Shisar. Thus, the Lehite *Shazer* refers either to the Arabian term for a water supply, or a clump of trees.[36]

In addition to the authentic ancient names mentioned above, other Book of Mormon names that don't appear in the English Bible but are attested in ancient Hebrew inscriptions include: Aha, Ammonihah, Chemish, Hagoth, Himni, Isabel, Jarom, Josh, Luram, Mathoni, Mathonihah, Muloki, and Sam.[37]

"It is no small feat," writes Nibley, "simply to have picked a lot of strange and original names out of the air. But what shall we say of the man who was able to pick the right ones?"[38]

24. "Without a Cause"

When Christ visited the Book of Mormon people in the ancient New World, he taught them many of the same things he had taught his disciples in the Old World. In Chapter 12 of 3 Nephi, for example, Christ gave a discourse that is nearly identical to the Sermon on the Mount in the New Testament. Critics claim that Joseph simply plagiarized the New Testament sermon. It is interesting to note, however, that there are *differences* between what we find in the New Testament and the Book of Mormon. For example, in Matthew 5:22 (the Sermon on the Mount), Christ said: "But I say unto you, That whosoever is angry with his brother without a cause shall be in danger of the judgment." In 3 Nephi 12:22 Christ said: "But I say unto you, that whosoever is angry with his brother shall be in danger of his judgment." The astute reader will notice that in 3 Nephi the words "without a cause" are absent.

When we examine the earliest Greek copies of the New Testament—documents that were discovered after Joseph Smith had died—we find that the phrase "without a cause" is also generally absent. As Professor John Welch notes, the verse in 3 Nephi discourages all anger whereas the verse in Matthew permits justifiable anger.

"The former is more like the demanding sayings of Jesus regarding committing adultery in one's heart (see Matthew 5:28) and loving one's enemies (see v. 44), neither of which offers the disciple a convenient loophole of self-justification or rationalization."[39]

Some non-LDS scholars believe that "without a cause" was added to Matthew 5:22 in an attempt to reflect a Semitic idiom that does not allow just anger under any circumstance. The King James Bible's "without a cause" however, implies that anger is okay when there is cause, while the Book of Mormon more accurately reflects the likely original intention of the passage.[40] The fact that Joseph Smith got it right, when no scholars in his world would have been aware of the later Greek insertion, shouldn't be amazing—but it is.

NOTES

1. LaRoy Sunderland, *Mormonism Exposed and Refuted* (New York: Piercy and Reed, 1838), 47.

2. Wayne A. Larsen, Alvin C. Rencher, and Tim Layton, "Multiple Authorship in the Book of Mormon," *New Era,* Nov. 1979, 10.

3. Wayne A. Larsen, Alvin C. Rencher, and Tim Layton, "Who Wrote the Book of Mormon? An Analysis of Wordprints," *BYU Studies* 20, no. 3 (Spring 1980): 227.

4. Ibid., 245.

5. John Hilton, "On Verifying Wordprint Studies: Book of Mormon Authorship," *BYU Studies* 30, no. 3 (Summer 1990): 101.

6. John W. Welch, "Chiasmus in the Book of Mormon," *BYU Studies* 10, no. 1 (Autumn 1969): 77.

7. "Chiasmus in Helaman 6:7–13," *Reexploring the Book of Mormon,* ed. John W. Welch, 230–31.

8. Daniel C. Peterson, "Editor's Introduction: Not So Easily Dismissed: Some Facts for Which Counterexplanations of the Book of Mormon Will Need to Account," *The FARMS Review* 17, no. 2 (2005): xxx.

9. These examples are given in Angela Crowell, "Hebraisms in the Book of Mormon," *The Zarahemla Record* (Summer and Fall 1982), 2.

10. John A. Tvedtnes, "Hebraisms in the Book of Mormon: A Preliminary Survey," *BYU Studies* 11, no. 1 (Autumn 1970): 53.

11. Ibid., 51.

12. David P. Wright, " 'In Plain Terms that We May Understand': Joseph

Smith's Transformation of Hebrews in Alma 12–13," *New Approaches to the Book of Mormon: Explorations in Critical Methodology,* ed. Brent L. Metcalfe (Salt Lake City, UT: Signature Books, 1993), 165 n2.

13. Sidney B. Sperry, "The Book of Mormon as Translation English," *Improvement Era,* Mar. 1935, 188.

14. Ibid., 187.

15. Tvedtnes, "Hebraisms in the Book of Mormon," 51.

16. Mark Twain (Samuel L. Clemens), *Roughing It* (Hartford, CT: American Publishing, 1899), 128; at http://etext.lib.virginia.edu/etcbin/toccer-new2?id=TwaRoug.sgm&images=images/modeng&data=/texts/english/modeng/parsed&tag=public&part=16&division=div1 (accessed 25 October 2006).

17. Latayne Colvett Scott, *The Mormon Mirage: A Former Mormon Tells Why She Left the Church* (Grand Rapids, MI: Zondervan Publishing House, 1979), 63.

18. Brant A. Gardner, *Second Witness: Analytical and Contextual Commentary on the Book of Mormon,* 6 vols. (Salt Lake City, UT: Greg Kofford Books, 2007) 1:24; Nibley, *Since Cumorah,* 169.

19. Sunderland, *Mormonism Exposed and Refuted,* 43.

20. John A. Tvedtnes and Stephen D. Ricks, "Jewish and Other Semitic Texts Written in Egyptian Characters," *Journal of Book of Mormon Studies* 5, no. 2 (1996): 157–63.

21. John Gee, "A Note on the Name Nephi," *Journal of Book of Mormon Studies* 1, no. 1 (1992): 190–91.

22. Jeffrey R. Chadwick, "Sariah in the Elephantine Papyri," *Pressing Forward with the Book of Mormon: The FARMS Updates of the 1990s,* eds., John W. Welch and Melvin J. Thorne (Provo, UT: FARMS, 1999), 6.

23. John A. Tvedtnes, John Gee, and Matthew Roper, "Book of Mormon Names Attested in Ancient Hebrew Inscriptions," *Journal of Book of Mormon Studies* 9, no. 10 (2000): 45.

24. Terrence L. Szink, "Further Evidence of a Semitic Alma," *Journal of Book of Mormon Studies* 8, no. 1 (1999): 70.

25. Robert F. Smith, "New Information about Mulek, Son of the King," *Reexploring the Book of Mormon,* 142–44.

26. Hugh Nibley, *Lehi in the Desert and the World of the Jaredites: There Were Jaredites* (Salt Lake City, UT: Deseret Book; Provo: FARMS, 1988), 189–90.

27. Rev. M. T. Lamb, *The Golden Bible* (New York: Ward & Drummond, 1887), 303.

28. Nibley, *Lehi in the Desert,* 42.

29. Hugh Nibley, *An Approach to the Book of Mormon* (Salt Lake City, UT: Deseret Book, 1978), 234.

30. Nibley, *Lehi in the Desert,* 26.

31. Ibid, 27–28.

32. Ibid., 33–34.

33. Nibley, *An Approach to the Book of Mormon,* 232.

34. Ibid., 239.

35. Ibid., 232.

36. Nibley, *Lehi in the Wilderness,* 78–79.

37. Tvedtnes, Gee, and Roper, "Ancient Names Attested in Ancient Hebrew Inscriptions," 43.

38. Hugh Nibley, "The Book of Mormon as a Mirror of the East," *Improvement Era,* Nov. 1970, 125.

39. John W. Welch, "A Steady Stream of Significant Recognitions," *Echoes and Evidences of the Book of Mormon,* 335.

40. Ibid.

Book of Mormon: Journey through the Old World

25. Axial Period

The Book of Mormon opens with Lehi prophesying to the unrighteous people at Jerusalem in about 600 BC. Modern research has since demonstrated that the sixth century BC was a time of unusual change and excitement. Some scholars have referred to the general era as an "Axial Period" in world history because it was a pivotal point around which history turns.[1] One non-LDS scholar, for instance, describes the sixth century BC as the heart of the "Axial Period" of world history: "The most extraordinary events are concentrated in this period. . . . In this age were born the fundamental categories within which we still think today, and the beginnings of the world religions, by which human beings still live, were created. The step into universality was taken in every sense."[2]

Some of history's greatest changes were taking place among the people of the world and Lehi and his followers were right in the center of it. This was unknown, of course, in Joseph's own day.

26. Laban and His "Fifty"

Shortly after heeding the Lord's command to depart into the wilderness, Lehi sent his sons back to Jerusalem to obtain the plates of brass from Laban. These plates contained Lehi's genealogy and the writings of the early prophets. When Nephi and his brothers asked Laban for the brass plates in trade for their silver and gold, Laban tried to kill them and he took away their possessions. After a narrow escape, Laman and Lemuel (Nephi's brothers) complained about the impossibility of their task because of Laban and his "fifty" (1 Nephi 3:31).

To modern readers this sounds like a small army indeed, but to those of the ancient Near East, the size of Laban's garrison fits neatly into Old World customs. As Nibley observes, "It would have been just as easy for the author of 1 Nephi to have said 'fifty thousand,' and made it really impressive."[3] Instead, however, Nephi and his brothers mention only fifty. Nephi goes on to note that the Lord is "mightier than Laban and his fifty, yea, or even than his tens of thousands" (1 Nephi 4:1).

According to Nibley, a permanent garrison in a big city of Lehi's day consisted of thirty to eighty men. For example, in a recently discovered letter of Nebuchadnezzar (a contemporary of Lehi), the king speaks of a garrison of "fifty." In Babylonia, a platoon in the army consisted of fifty men. In addition, this permanent unit was always called a "fifty" just as Nephi spoke of "Laban with his fifty."[4]

27. Killing Laban and the Oath of Zoram

Again Nephi attempted to secure the plates. This time, however, he found Laban lying drunk in the street. The spirit of the Lord commanded Nephi to slay Laban so that he could obtain the plates. At first Nephi hesitated—he had never killed a man before. Again the spirit commanded Nephi to slay Laban and said that it was "better that one man should perish than that a nation should dwindle and perish in unbelief." At last Nephi obeyed and grabbing Laban by the hair, cut off his head with his own sword (see 1 Nephi 4:11–18).

While modern Americans have expressed concern about Nephi's killing of Laban, in light of Near Eastern thought his actions are not unusual. Dr. Nibley recalls the reaction to the story by a class of several Arab students. Nibley had just retold the part where Nephi had killed Laban when one Arab student asked, "Why did this Nephi wait so *long* to cut off Laban's head?"[5]

Nibley goes on to note: "Laban was wearing armor, so the only chance of dispatching him quickly, painlessly, and safely was to cut off his head—the conventional treatment of criminals in the East, where beheading has always been by the sword, and where an executioner would be fined for failing to decapitate his victim at one clean stroke."[6]

After Nephi killed Laban, he donned the governor's robes and went to the treasury disguised as Laban, where he tricked Laban's servant, Zoram, into acquiring the brass plates. When Zoram discovered that Nephi was not Laban, Nephi gripped Zoram in a vice-like grip and swore into his ear, "as the Lord liveth, and as I live" that he would spare Zoram's life if he would only listen (1 Nephi 4:32). Upon hearing this simple phrase, Zoram followed Nephi without further problems.

Among the desert people, an oath is the one thing which is held as most sacred. Arabs generally will not break an oath, even if their lives are in jeopardy. Nearly all Arabs—whether nomad or city dweller—believed that oaths were sacred and served as powerful covenants between two parties. The most binding oaths were those sworn by the life of something. As Nibley explains, "The only oath more awful than 'by my life' or (less commonly) 'by the life of my head,' is the *wa hayat Allah,* 'by the life of God,' or 'as the Lord liveth,' the Arabic equivalent of the ancient Hebrew *hai Elohim.*"[7]

28. Unknown Arabia

How easy would it have been for a young man in 1830 to write a novel about the ancient Old World and have it stand up to scrutiny nearly two hundred years later? When Joseph translated the Book of Mormon—with a tale of Lehites departing the Old World on a journey through southern Arabia—the best scholars of his day knew little about the ancient world in which the Lehites traveled. The few bits of information available were generally wrong and almost consistently described Arabia as a barren wasteland. According to some authors, Arabia was so hot that animals were roasted on the plains and birds in the midair. The southern coast of Arabia was thought to be dismal and barren—nothing but rocky wall. It was said that not even a blade of grass could be grown along the coastline. Very few books mentioned any fertile regions in Arabia, and those that did, got the information wrong as well—describing fertile regions as producing rice, maize, and tropical fruits.[8]

If Joseph had written the Book of Mormon with information sponged from his environment, he would have turned to the so-called experts of his day. So inaccurate were the experts of 1830 America, however, that if Joseph *had sponged* their information he would have produced a book full of errors.

29. Trails

Lehi and his family lived in the wilderness for many years, most likely following trails which were previously known only in ancient times. Today, scholars are aware of ancient caravan routes along "Frankincense Trails" where traders traveled to bring frankincense and myrrh from the southern coast to inland cities. At least two of these trails run south along the Arabian Peninsula near the shore of the Red Sea. Nephi likewise tells us that after Lehi departed Jerusalem, "he came down by the borders *near* the shore of the Red Sea; and he traveled in the wilderness in the borders which are *nearer* the Red Sea" (1 Nephi 2:5; italics added).

These trails were well-traveled but were not well-defined narrow roadways (contrary to the image conjured by most modern readers). Instead, they were general routes that lead from water hole to water hole (and the water holes were typically guarded). Some of these trails could be a half mile to a dozen miles wide and travelers could pass by other people on the trail and never see them.[9] The fact that there really are trails that follow the route described by Nephi is one more hit that Joseph Smith got right.

30. Trail Names

While traveling through Arabia, Lehi would frequently rename rivers and valleys after the people in his party.

> And it came to pass that he called the name of the river, Laman . . . saying: O that thou might be like unto this river, continually running into the fountain of all righteousness!
>
> And he also spake unto Lemuel: O that thou mightest be like unto this valley, firm and steadfast, and immovable in keeping the commandments of the Lord!
>
> And it came to pass that my father did speak unto them in the

valley of Lemuel, with power, being filled with the Spirit. (1 Nephi 2:8,
9–10, 14)

Such a practice is foreign to Americans, as we see in the comments
of one critic who complained: "All the rivers and valleys he [Joseph
Smith] makes Lehi name with *new names*."[10] What a strange custom
indeed. In Lehi's world, however, it was customary among the Arabs to
rename any new territory you encountered with your own names. An
Arabian valley, for example, could have several different names at different points, according to who was traveling on the trail.[11]

31. Nephi's Bow

The Lehites' journey was frequently fraught with difficulties. Nephi,
for example, tells us that he used a "fine steel" bow to hunt for food. It
should first be noted that there is evidence that a "steel" bow in this passage actually refers to a double convex (snakelike) long range bow rather
than one actually made of "steel."[12]

Despite the high quality of Nephi's bow, however, it broke during
one leg of their journey. To make matters worse, his brothers' bows "lost
their springs" at about the same time. As LDS research Eugene England
has found, the general area of modern Jiddah—which is midway down
the eastern shore of the Red Sea—"is known for a combination of heat,
humidity, sand, and salt that rusts car fenders in a few months and turns
limber any dry wood brought from other areas."[13]

After their bows failed, Nephi found wood to construct new bows.
"Around Jiddah," notes England, "grows the pomegranate tree, excellent for bowmaking."[14] Not only did Nephi make new bows, but he also
made new arrows (1 Nephi 16:23). Why? As Near Eastern specialist Dr.
William Hamblin points out, his new wooden bow would need longer,
lighter arrows than his long-range bow.[15] As the popular saying goes,
"the devil is in the details." It's nothing less than amazing that Joseph
Smith got so many inconspicuous things right—things that go unnoticed but end up accurately reflecting an ancient world setting, just as the
Book of Mormon claims.

32. Tree of Life, Part 1

While the Lehites traveled through Arabia, Lehi had a vision of the tree of life. In the vision, a man dressed in a white robe led Lehi to a dreary waste. After traveling for what seemed like several hours in darkness, he came to a large field where he saw a tree bearing an exceedingly white fruit that was delicious to the soul. Lehi wanted his family to partake of the fruit as well and called to them. Lehi's wife, Sariah, and his sons Sam and Nephi came and partook of the fruit, but Lehi's wayward sons, Laman and Lemuel, would not.

Lehi spoke of seeing a rod of iron that extended along the bank of a river and led to the tree of life. A straight and narrow path ran alongside this iron rod and also led to the tree. Scores of people were pressing forward toward the path that led to the tree. As they followed the path, however, many became lost in a mist of darkness. Some of the people grabbed hold of the iron rod and hung on through the darkness until they reached the tree.

On the other side of the river stood a large building filled with well-dressed people mocking those who partook of the fruit on the tree. Some of the people who had partaken of the fruit became ashamed and deserted the tree for the building. Some of them drowned in the river, others became hopelessly lost, and still others joined those in the building—mocking those who ate the fruit on the tree (see 1 Nephi 8).

Not many years ago, while attending Duke University, Mormon scholar John Welch participated in a graduate seminar on early Christian writings, when the professor began to discuss a little-known writing entitled the *Narrative of Zosimus*. This narrative—written in Hebrew and dating to about the time of Christ or earlier—purports to tell a tale that could date to Lehi's day. The story, notes Welch,

> tells of a righteous family that God had led away from Jerusalem prior to its destruction by the Babylonians around 600 BC and how this group escaped to a land of blessedness where they kept records on metal plates soft enough that they could inscribe them with their fingernails. In the story, Zosimus was allowed to visit these people in vision. In order to get to their land, Zosimus had to journey through the wilderness, pass through impenetrable mists of darkness, cross the ocean, and come to a tree that bore pure fruit and gave forth water sweet as honey. (See the same elements in 1 Nephi 8:10–12 and 11:25.)[16]

There is no evidence that the *Narrative of Zosimus* was known in an English-speaking land prior to the publication of the Book of Mormon. The first known modern reappearance of the narrative was a Russian translation from an Old Church Slavonic text dating to the 1870s (almost fifty years after the Book of Mormon was published).[17]

The story of Lehi's vision and the Narrative of Zosimus are not 100 percent identical (which would only be the case if one was a direct copy of the other). But there are some amazing similarities that seem to rule out coincidence. The striking similarities they share include metaphors, specific words, phrases, and images:

> The many parallels between the early chapters of the Book of Mormon and this Narrative require little elaboration: dwelling in the desert, being led by prayer and faith, wandering through a dark and dreary waste, being caught away to the bank of a river, crossing to the other side of a river or abyss and passing through a great mist, coming to a tree whose fruit is most sweet above all, eating and drinking from the tree which was also a fountain of living waters, being greeted by an escort, being interrogated as to desires, beholding a vision of the Son of God, keeping records on soft metal plates, recording the history of a group of people who escaped the destruction of Jerusalem at the time of Jeremiah, being led to a land of promise and of great abundance due to righteousness, practicing constant prayer, living in chastity, receiving revelations concerning the wickedness of the people of Jerusalem, and yet obtaining assurances of the mercy to be extended to the inhabitants of Jerusalem.[18]

One parallel or perhaps two might have been a lucky guess on Joseph's part, but such numerous parallels indicate some sort of connection between the Book of Mormon and the world from which it claims to have derived. From where did Joseph Smith learn these things? Outside of the possibility that both Lehi and Zosimus shared similar revelations, Mormon scholars are still attempting to determine just what relationship exists between the two narratives. Two theories have been suggested: (1) Perhaps Lehi made contact with others in their Arabian journey and shared the tale of his vision; or (2) some ancient source or tradition influenced both the *Narrative of Zosimus* as well as Lehi's vision.[19] If the Book of Mormon is really based on an authentic ancient text with Near Eastern roots, it should have at least some stories that are similar to what we find in other documents from the same period. Indeed, this is what we now find in other Old World traditions.

Within recent years other similar motifs have been discovered—dating from the fifth century BC to the AD third century—in Italy, Sicily, Crete, and Macedonia. These motifs depict the dead wandering through a world of darkness in search of a white cypress tree. Non-Mormon commentators agree that the cypress tree represents the tree of life. These same commentators agree that this mythology most likely originated in Egypt.

British scholar Margaret Barker (who is a Methodist preacher and president of the Society for Old Testament Study) says that according to ancient traditions, the tree of life "made one happy," and the fruit on the tree is described as "beautiful, fiery," and much "like white grapes."[20] She says, "I do not know of any other source that describes the fruit as white grapes. Image my surprise when I read the account of Lehi's vision of the tree whose *white fruit* made one happy."[21]

As to the rod of iron, Barker notes that rods in the Bible typically represent rulership. She believes a more accurate symbol of the rod is as a tool to guide or lead—as we find among shepherds. "Lehi's vision," she notes, "has the iron rod *guiding* people to the great tree." This, she explains, is "the older and probably the original understanding of the word [rod]."[22]

Dr. C. Wilfred Griggs (professor of Ancient Scripture) notes:

> The Book of Mormon brought the tree of life to our attention long before modern scholarship revealed how common the tree was in ancient history. The symbol of that tree pervades the art and literature of every Mediterranean culture from centuries before the time of Lehi until well after the time of Moroni. This fact, and the fact that Lehi and Nephi portrayed the spiritual meaning of that symbol much the same way other ancient cultures portrayed it, demonstrate that the Book of Mormon is an ancient text, not an invention of the nineteenth-century social milieu.[23]

33. Nephi and His Asherah

Despite most people's perception of the ancient Israelites, modern scholars recognize that the Israelites were not typically monotheistic (they didn't believe in a single God). For many years under the reign of the Judges, many Israelites worshipped a female virgin deity—a consort to God—by the name of Asherah. Some biblical scholars believe that Jeremiah—a contemporary prophet of Lehi—mocked and denounced Asherah worship. After Jerusalem fell to the Babylonians (right after the Lehites fled Jerusalem) and was restored under the prophet Ezra, Asherah worship finally ended. This means that Lehi and his son Nephi would undoubtedly have been familiar with Asherah.

Why do we know so little about this consort of God? In about 600 BC, once Judaism became opposed to Asherah worship, reforming Deuteronomist priests filtered and reshaped the Bible and effectively removed most reference and details of this female deity. Hints remain, but there is little surviving text that teaches us about her character or nature.

So popular and important was Asherah during Israelite history, however, that "an image or symbol of Asherah stood in Solomon's temple at Jerusalem for nearly two-thirds of its existence."[24] The image had a female body from the waist up and a single column from the waist down. This depiction represented her maternal, nourishing, and nurturing powers in the upper half of the image, whereas the single column below her waist represented a tree trunk. Asherah was associated with the sacred tree—the Tree of Life. She was, in fact, considered to *be* the tree of life. Likewise, the Menorah—the seven-branched candle that stood for centuries in the Jerusalem temple—is said to represent a stylized almond tree which, at certain points in its life cycle, was *radiantly* white. The Greek word *almond* likely derives from a Hebrew term that means "Great Mother."[25]

What does this have to do with Nephi and the Book of Mormon? In 1 Nephi chapter 8, Lehi has a vision of a tree that bears beautiful fruit that gladdens the soul. Nephi wants to more fully understand what his father saw and prays for his own vision. In chapter 11, we read of Nephi's vision and the things that he saw—including the sacred tree. Nephi is guided through the vision by a "spirit" or angel who asks Nephi what he desires. "To know the interpretation thereof," replies Nephi. Instead of answering Nephi directly, the Spirit shows Nephi more things in the vision (1 Nephi 11:4–22).

"And it came to pass that I looked and beheld the great city of Jerusalem, and also other cities. And I beheld the city of Nazareth; and in the city of Nazareth I beheld a virgin, and she was exceedingly fair and white" (v. 13).

The Spirit asks Nephi what he sees. "A virgin, most beautiful and fair above all other virgins" (vv. 14–15) Nephi replies.

"Knowest thou the condescension of God?" (v. 16) asks the Spirit.

Nephi responds: "I know that he loveth his children; nevertheless, I do not know the meaning of all things" (v. 17).

"The virgin whom thou seest," explains the Spirit, "is the mother of the Son of God, after the manner of the flesh." The Spirit then carries Nephi away for a space of time and returns to show the virgin holding a baby. "Behold the Lamb of God, yea, even the Son of the Eternal Father!" (vv. 18–21).

So in response to Nephi's question to know the interpretation of the tree of life, the Spirit shows Nephi Mary and then the baby Jesus. There is nothing discussed about trees or fruit, yet the Spirit asks, "Knowest thou the meaning of the tree which thy father saw?" (v. 21).

To which Nephi responds: "Yea, it is the love of God, which sheddeth itself abroad in the hearts of the children of men; wherefore, it is the most desirable above all things" (v. 22).

What young adult in Jacksonian America (or modern America for that matter) would make a connection between a sacred tree and the Virgin Mary? In Nephi and Lehi's day, however, the connection would have been obvious (and obviously colored by their cultural background). Mary was a perfect mortal typification of Asherah—she was a virgin, fair ("white"), and the mother of the most joyous thing in the world. While Mary is not Asherah, to Nephi the symbolism would have made sense and would have taught him not only of the coming of the Christ, but also would have helped him understand the meaning of the sacred tree. It's easy to see how Nephi's culture would have prepared him to understand such an interpretation in his vision as recorded in 1 Nephi 11. But how did Joseph Smith know this in 1830?[26]

Methodist scholar Margaret Barker recently noted some of the interesting parallels between the tree of life in Nephi's vision and ancient Near Eastern traditions—including the fact that both contain the symbolism of the tree as the Heavenly Mother—in Nephi's vision this tree was represented by Mary. "This revelation to Joseph Smith," she said, was the ancient Mother symbolism, "intact, and almost certainly as it was known in 600 BCE."[27]

34. The Liahona

During the Lehites sojourn through the Arabian wilderness, Lehi was given a device, called the "Liahona," which helped guide them on their journey. Nephi described the Liahona as round, made of brass, and containing two spindles or arrows (1 Nephi 16:10). Nephi called the ball a "compass" (1 Nephi 18:12) and mentions that there were things written in the Liahona which gave them instructions (1 Nephi 16:27, 29). The most important aspect of the Liahona was that it worked according to faith and righteousness. Unlike a typical mariner's compass—which indicates the direction to magnetic north—the Liahona indicated the direction Lehi should go.

While critics often claim that the compass (by which they mean a mariner's compass) was unknown in Lehi's day, it's important to note that the function of magnetic hematite—the principal core of iron—was well understood in both the Old and New Worlds before Lehi left Jerusalem. "Magnetite, or *lodestone,* is, of course, naturally magnetic iron, and the word *magnetite* comes from the name of a place in which it was mined in Asia Minor by at least the seventh century BC, namely Magnesia."[28]

If the compass was known in parts of the Old and New Worlds at such early dates, it does not seem out of line to believe that Nephi might also have understood the nature of a magnetic compass.

The word *compass,* however, has two basic meanings: 1) to move together—always referring to a pair of things in motion; 2) to enclose, embrace, step completely, circle, or round. This second definition refers to the motion of making a circle. Either way, the word *compass* could correctly refer to the Liahona because of its round (ball) shape or the motion of the arrows.[29]

The Liahona compass also fits neatly into Old World traditions. Dr. Nibley once pointed to an article written by non-LDS scholar T. Fahd who, in 1958, published his research on the study of belomancy—or "the practice of divination by shooting, tossing, shaking, or otherwise manipulating rods, darts, pointers, or other sticks, all originally derived from arrows."[30] According to Fahd, pre-Islamic Arabs consulted the Lord by tossing or manipulating pointers. Fahd claims that inscriptions on the pointers would often provide travel directions. Sometimes the divination arrows were carried in a special container when taken on trips.[31]

35. Nahom

In 1 Nephi chapter 7, not long after their departure into the wilderness, Nephi and his brothers return to Jerusalem to bring Ishmael (a righteous friend) and his daughters (which later become the wives of Lehi's sons). In chapter 16 Ishmael died during their journey through the Arabian Peninsula and in verse 34 we read that Ishmael was buried "in the place that was *called* Nahom." As noted before, the Lehites typically gave new names to the places through which they traveled. In this instance, however, we read that Ishmael's burial spot "was called Nahom"—which implies that this was the name of the location prior to the Lehites' arrival.

In the late twentieth century, a non-LDS German archaeological team was excavating an ancient temple in southern Arabia when they discovered the inscription of a man belonging to the tribe of NHM. A few years later, two more altars from the same excavation were also found to contain the tribal inscription of NHM. Since this area had been utilized for more than 2500 years (and was actively used during the day of Lehi), non-LDS scholars have suggested that—in typical Near Eastern fashion—NHM was not only a tribal name, but the name of a territory in which this tribe lived.[32]

Ancient Hebrew did not use vowels, so NHM could be translated with the use of various vowel sounds including Nahom as found in the Book of Mormon. Even if it was translated as Nehem, or Naham, however, the meaning is the same. Nephi didn't use English characters. He would have recorded what they heard—what the place was called—which was then recorded in a reformed Egyptian script and eventually transliterated into Roman letters for our English Book of Mormon text. Recently discovered ancient maps, for example (which would have been unavailable to Joseph Smith), show a location—in this same spot in Arabia—that went by the name of Nehem (other maps spell the location as Nihm, Nehem, and even Naham, but they all refer to the same geographical location in southern Arabia).

Another layer to this parallel is added when we discover that the Semitic root for NHM means to "comfort" or to "console" (as in consoling someone that is grieving) and that Nephi points out that when Ishmael was buried at Nahom, Ishmael's daughters did "mourn exceedingly" (1 Nephi 16:35).[33] The layers to this parallel compounds exponentially when we recognize that NHM was the largest burial site in all of ancient Arabia and that starting in about 600 BC (the same time that the Lehites fled Jerusalem) that anyone could be buried there.[34]

Some might be tempted to chalk up the name NHM as a mere coincidence to the Book of Mormon's "Nahom." The likelihood of coincidence diminishes, however, when we examine the location of the southern Arabian NHM. For over three decades many LDS scholars have argued that the Lehites followed ancient frankincense trails down to southern Arabia (see section 28 in this book). These trails led from water hole to water hole—something the Lehites would have required in order to survive. After Ishmael's burial at Nahom, Nephi says that they turned "eastward from that time forth" (1 Nephi 17:1). While this eastward turn doesn't show up in any anciently known source, we find that such an eastward turn in the frankincense trail actually exists right in the area of NHM. Still adding to the depth of this parallel, we find that this eastward turn leads to a fertile area on the coast of the Arabian Peninsula where a ship could be built and launched.

36. Raw Meat

After turning east at Nahom and continuing their journey to Bountiful, we read that the Lehites suffered many afflictions and had to live on "raw meat" because they were not to make fire frequently (1 Nephi 17:2). To help them, the Lord made their raw meat "sweet" (v. 12). In 1887 one critic wrote:

> After a very careful study of the book [Book of Mormon], a conscientious and painstaking examination of all the evidences he has been able to gather both for and against it, the author of these pages has been forced to reject every one of the [book's] . . . claims.
>
> There was no lack of wood for fire in the wilderness, no lack of stones to smite together, but simply to prove to them that they are the Lord's special pets, he saves them the trouble of making fire by performing the prodigious miracle of making raw meat sweet and palatable.[35]

We shouldn't fault a critic in 1887 for finding this strange—little was known about ancient Arabia when the critic made this charge. What do we know today? Dr. Nibley quotes explorers who have traveled through Arabia and were afraid of marauding raiders. They dared not build open fires for fear of attracting the attention of bandits.[36]

Near Eastern archaeologist Dr. Jeffery Chadwick sees things a little differently. According to Chadwick, the Lehites probably didn't make much fire because of the lack of firewood and kindling (or the inconsistency of such finds), and because they probably traveled in the cool of the night and rested during the day when no fires for visibility were needed.[37] Both Chadwick and Nibley agree, however, that no fire meant the Lehites enjoyed few cooked foods—including meat.

According to Nibley's investigations, many of the desert travelers ate goat and sheep kidney raw—with a bit of salt. Others ate entire slices of flesh raw. One ancient traveler tells how the Bedouins would slaughter a camel and eat its raw meat or scorch it quickly over a small fire.

Chadwick explains that local fruits, vegetables, and cheeses would have been available so the only meat that would have needed cooking would have been directly after a hunt. They may have cooked meat occasionally, but that would have satisfied only a single meal. The majority of the meat would have been sun dried while raw, without cooking it.[38] He continues, "In other words, the 'raw meat' that the party ate would have been what we today call jerky. And it, too, was probably seasoned so that it was 'sweet, that ye cook it not.' Jerky travels well, even in hot desert terrain, as does cheese and bread. So the party could have maintained an adequate food supply on their trail without having to 'make much fire.' "[39]

In either Nibley or Chadwick's scenario, the actions of the Lehites and their eating of "raw meat" are consistent with what we now know about ancient Arabian travelers.

37. Bountiful

After a long journey that probably took several years, the Lehites finally came to Bountiful—a land of "much fruit and also wild honey" (1 Nephi 17:5). Here they camped and built a ship for the final leg of their journey to the Americas. One twentieth-century critic (who claims a PhD in biology) argued that the Book of Mormon's description of Bountiful is proof that the book is fraudulent: "Arabia is bountiful in sunshine, petroleum, sand, heat and fresh air, but certainly not in 'much fruit and also wild honey,' nor has it been since Pleistocene times. 1 Nephi 18:1 indicates that the Jews made a ship from ample timber of Arabia. The same objection applies here also."[40]

It's really no surprise that critics would laugh at the Book of Mormon's description of a fertile region on the coast of southern Arabia. As noted in Section 27, during Joseph Smith's day even the best American scholars thought that Arabia's southern coastline was a dismal, barren place. Modern scholarship, however, is aware of a few locations on Oman's southern Dohfar coast (on the southeast end of the Arabian Peninsula), where matches to the Book of Mormon's Bountiful are striking.

According to the Book of Mormon, Bountiful was a fertile place with fruit and honey, shipbuilding timber, flint deposits for making tools, and a nearby mount where Nephi's brothers nearly threw Nephi into the sea (see 1 Nephi 17 for such details). Located precisely where we would expect to find Bountiful is the Arabian site of Khor Kharfot—the most naturally fertile location on the Arabian coast. There are fresh water springs, timber trees up to forty feet in circumference, wild honey, and small game animals. Until recently, there was a sheltered sea inlet from where one could launch a raft (it is now closed by a sand bar), and towering on the west side of the bay is a mount where Nephi could have prayed, and 120-foot cliffs where Nephi's brothers could have threatened to throw off their younger brother.

Geologists have recently found nearby iron deposit and forms of flint from which Nephi could have fashioned tools. All the items necessary to meet the description of Bountiful is found on the Dohfar coast just as described in the Book of Mormon.[41]

38. Ancient Shipbuilding

As the Lehites traveled to southern Arabia they would have passed several seaports where ships could be observed. Only recently have historians become aware that "centuries before Lehi's day, Oman [on Arabia's southern coast] was at the forefront of Arab sea exploration and trade, building ships that operated to Africa, India, and China."[42] The Lehites' vessel, however, was not constructed "after the manner of men" (18:2). Instead, the Lord showed Nephi how to build the ship (1 Nephi 17:8) and to work timbers of "curious workmanship" (18:1).

What did this ship look like? The fact that the Lehites went "down into the ship" (1 Nephi 18:5–6) and danced on board (v. 9), suggests a decked vessel. We also know that they must have had a sail since the ship was driven by the wind (vv. 8–9), and it must have had a rudder since they were able to steer (v. 13).

Most of the ships at Arabian ports would have been hulled ships—shaped like most people would imagine a ship or boat. The boards of a hulled ship would be lashed together—a laborious process that takes a long time and great skill to make with the precision necessary to create a seaworthy vessel. Nephi, however, says that their ship was *not* "after the manner of men." A large *raft* would have been easier to construct but would have required more timber—which made such vessels uncommon, if not unfamiliar, among Arabian seamen. At Kharfot, however—and significantly *only* at Kharfot—the availability of timber was a nonissue.

A large raft would have offered several advantages to the Lehites. They are not very fast, but less destructible. And they offer greater stability during storms because of a broader keel. A raft would have been like a floating warehouse with greater deck space or even multiple decks and private quarters (which is what we find in raft vessels in non-Arabian cultures). It also would have required less skill in maneuvering and launching.[43]

From Oman, the Lehites would have sailed east, island hopping along the way, and stopping frequently for repairs as well as to replenish supplies, food, and fresh water. The trip could easily have taken a year before they reached the Americas.

39. Transoceanic Crossings

A growing number of non-LDS scholars believe that the Americas were populated—at least in part—by groups who sailed from the Old World. In a 1985 article in *Archaeology,* for instance, E. James Dixon explained that some of the most ancient early American sites were in South America—contrary to what one would expect if all ancient Americans had first arrived by way of the Bering Strait (near Alaska). "According to this line of reasoning, early humans first entered the Americas by transoceanic voyages across the Pacific Ocean from Asia" and then would have "gradually spread northward from there." He suggests that anciently, there may have been "numerous contacts, and probably even population movements across the Pacific between Asia and North America."[44]

Studies indicate ancient sailors landed in the Americas both intentionally and accidentally. "The winds and currents from the Strait of Gibraltar," notes non-LDS scholar George Carter, "drive directly to America with great steadiness. Any mariner venturing out to sea beyond the ancient Pillars of Hercules and not having any mishap would arrive in America in a very short time."[45]

In 1969, the famous non-Mormon explorer Thor Heyerdahl attempted to show that the Atlantic Ocean had been crossed by early man. A papyrus boat, which he named *Ra I,* was built by Buduma boat builders from Chad in Central Africa and launched from the ancient Phoenician port of Saff in Morocco. After three thousand miles of travel, the *Ra I* finally broke apart before reaching the New World. The following year, Heyerdahl tried again—this time having learned from his mistakes—and the *Ra II* was built by the South American Aymara Indians from Lake Titicaca (the world's highest navigatable lake). This time his ship made it. Heyerdahl points out several similarities between the Old and New Worlds and believes that ancient contacts between the two worlds had occurred. He once said: "Although I am not a member of the Mormon faith, I must admit that some of the discoveries that I have made on the Polynesian islands and in South America would conform with the contents of the Book of Mormon."[46]

Non-Mormon scholar Norman Totten explains that Heyerdahl's adventures were just a few among several voyages which have shown that the ancients could very well have crossed the oceans. Other modern researchers have crossed the Atlantic in kayaks, dugouts, rafts, and reed boats. One scholar documented about a hundred accidental landings of Japanese fishing boats on American shores prior to 1850. Of these accidental landings, the surviving Japanese sailors were almost always absorbed into the local Indian populations.[47]

There are many evidences for contact between the ancient Old and New Worlds. Some of those evidences are cultural, linguistic, and botanical. Critics typically dismiss cultural similarities as simply evidence of independent invention. Since humans are equally intelligent all over the global, when faced with similar challenges, they often invent similar things. While there is truth to such a claim, botanical evidence cannot be reproduced by independent means.

For example, not too many years ago a mural depicting a pineapple was found on a wall from ancient Pompeii (which was buried under volcanic ash at the end of the AD first century).[48] Pineapples are not native to Naples, yet somehow the artists in Pompeii knew of the pineapple before, it was believed, men had sailed to the Americas. The only explanation for such a find is that men had sailed to (or from) the Americas in ancient times and had returned with either a pineapple—or the description of a pineapple—from which the artist rendered his mural.

George Carter also points out that the ancient Romans recorded the "appearance of a new grain" that grew "on a stalk like sugarcane but bears grain in an ear," and the individual grains, they noted, were "as large as peas."[49] This description certainly refers to maize (American corn), which not only didn't grow anciently in the Old World, but—because of sophisticated agricultural techniques—does not grow wild anywhere. The corn had to have come from a New World farm.

In 1929 a map was found in Constantinople (dating from 1513) which gave the correct longitudinal placement of South America and Africa. The creator of the map wrote that his map was based on other maps, some of which dated to 330 BC.[50] George Carter, a Catholic ancient America expert and professor of the Department of Geography at Texas A & M has written:

> Mountains of evidence that the people of America learned from transoceanic travelers have been put forward intermittently for over a century. But such observations have always been knocked down by the argument that because anyone can invent anything, cultural parallels are simply classic cases of independent invention. That, of course, was my opinion until the plant evidence was thrust upon me. For the independent invention argument fails completely when one is dealing with biological items.[51]

Carter discovered that there was an abundance of biological evidence for transoceanic crossings. "Only God," he notes, "can make a sweet potato (peanut, maize, chicken, hibiscus). The list is now becoming very long."[52] The independent invention theory may be debated when considering man-made objects, but not with God-made or biological creations. Man cannot invent a sweet potato, or a chicken, or a peanut. In order for such items to appear in areas where they are not naturally grown, they would have to be brought from places where they are naturally grown. Most scholars have traditionally believed that chickens, for example, were first introduced to the Americas by Columbus. Other scholars, however, have disputed this claim. Carter points out, for instance, "The Indians do not have the races of chickens that they would have if the Spanish alone had brought them. They have chickens that are appropriate for Asiatic introductions."[53]

A recent discovery of ancient chickens bone in Chili may have put the chicken question to rest. DNA studies of the Chili chicken bones show a rare mutation that can only have come from chickens of the Polynesian Islands. Mason Inman, writing for National Geographic, tells of the finding: "This means Polynesians not only colonized nearly every island in the South Pacific—making journeys over thousands of miles—but they also made the long hop all the way to the Americas."[54]

Space prohibits a full listing of biological items that could only have been brought from across the seas, but a second item noted by other scholars is cotton. According to botanists, the ancient Andean (New World) cotton was a hybrid of wild American cotton and domesticated

Old World cotton such as that grown in Egypt. How did domesticated cotton reach the New World in ancient times? Cold kills cotton so it could not have come via the Bering Strait. Water kills cotton so it could not have floated by ocean currents. Birds didn't carry it because they detest the cotton ball and its seeds.[55] Therefore, many botanists have concluded that domesticated Old World cotton came by ship, in approximately 2000 BC, from the Old to the New World.[56] To sum up the impact of these evidences, we quote Carter: "The plant and the chicken evidence proves in absolute terms that the great oceans were crossed, very early, and seemingly fairly easily, for plants and animals were carried so easily that they did not have to be eaten. I [Carter] consider that the biological data has proved the case for diffusion. This, then, changes the odds and makes more admissible all the cultural evidence."[57]

NOTES

1. Nibley, *Since Cumorah,* 270–71.
2. Nibley, *An Approach to the Book of Mormon,* vii.
3. Nibley, *Lehi in the Desert,* 97.
4. Ibid., 97–98.
5. Nibley, *An Approach to the Book of Mormon,* viii.
6. Nibley, *Lehi in the Desert,* 101.
7. Ibid., 103.
8. Eugene England, "Through the Arabian Desert to a Bountiful Land: Could Joseph Smith Have Known the Way?" *Book of Mormon Authorship: New Light on Ancient Origins,* ed., Noel B. Reynolds (Provo, UT: Brigham Young University Religious Studies Center, 1982), 143–56.
9. Lynn M. and Hope A. Hilton, "In Search of Lehi's Trail—Part 1: The Preparation," *Ensign,* Sept. 1976, 44.
10. John Hyde Jun., *Mormonism: Its Leaders & Designs* (New York: W. P. Fetridge & Co., 1857), 223; italics in original.
11. Nibley, *Lehi in the Desert,* 75.
12. Kevin Barney, "On Nephi's Steel Bow," (20 February 2006) at http://www.bycommonconsent.com/2006/02/on-nephis-steel-bow/ (accessed 4 July 2008).
13. England, *Through the Arabian Desert to a Bountiful Land,* 151.

14. Ibid.

15. William J. Hamblin, "Nephi's Bows and Arrows," *Reexploring the Book of Mormon,* 41–42.

16. John W. Welch, "A Book You Can Respect," *Ensign,* Sept. 1977, 48.

17. John W. Welch, "The Narrative of Zosimus and the Book of Mormon," *BYU Studies* 22, no. 3 (Summer 1982): 311–13.

18. Ibid., 314.

19. Ibid., 27–28.

20. Margaret Barker, "Joseph Smith and Preexilic Israelite Religion," *The Worlds of Joseph Smith: A Bicentennial Conference at the Library of Congress* (a special issue of *BYU Studies* 44, no. 4 [2005]), 76.

21. Ibid.

22. Ibid., 77.

23. C. Wilfred Griggs, "The Tree of Life in Ancient Cultures," *Ensign,* June 1988, 27.

24. Daniel C. Peterson, "Nephi and His Asherah," *Journal of Book of Mormon Studies* 9, no. 2 (2000): 19.

25. Ibid., 19, 22

26. Ibid., 22

27. Margaret Barker, "Joseph Smith and Preexilic Israelite Religion," 76.

28. Robert F. Smith, "Lodestone and the Liahona," *Reexploring the Book of Mormon,* 45.

29. Nibley, *Since Cumorah,* 296.

30. Ibid., 287.

31. Hugh W. Nibley, "Howlers in the Book of Mormon," *The Prophetic Book of Mormon,* 244–45.

32. S. Kent Brown, "New Light from Arabia on Lehi's Trail," *Echoes and Evidences,* 82; S. Kent Brown, "The Place that was Called Nahom: New Light from Ancient Yemen," *Journal of Book of Mormon Studies* 8, no. 1 (1999): 66–68; Warren P. Aston, "Newly Found Altars from Nahom," *Journal of Book of Mormon Studies* 10, no. 2 (2001): 57–61.

33. Hilton and Hilton, "In Search of Lehi's Trail—Part 1: The Preparation," 12–13; Nibley, *Lehi in the Desert,* 79.

34. Warren P. Aston, "Across Arabia With Lehi and Sariah: 'Truth Shall Spring out of the Earth,' " *Journal of Book of Mormon Studies* 15, no. 2 (2006): 15; Peter Johnson, "A Journey of Faith: Trapped in the Land of Lehi on 9/11," at http://meridianmagazine.com/arts/020925yemen.html (accessed 13 December 2006).

35. Lamb, *The Golden Bible,* 11, 61.

36. Nibley, *Lehi in the Desert,* 63–64.

37. Jeffrey R. Chadwick, "An Archaeologist's View," *Journal of Book of Mormon Studies* 15, no. 2 (2006): 74.

38. Nibley, *Lehi in the Desert,* 64.

39. Chadwick, "An Archaeologist's View," 74.

40. Thomas D. S. Key, *A Biologist Examines The Book of Mormon* (Bainbridge, Georgia, undated), 1.

41. Aston, "Newly Found Altars from Nahom," 16–17.

42. Ibid., 22

43. Ibid., 23.

44. E. James Dixon, "The Origins of the First Americans," *Archaeology* (March/April 1985), 26–27.

45. George F. Carter, "Before Columbus," *The Book of Mormon: The Keystone Scripture,* ed., Paul R. Cheesman (Provo, UT: BYU Religious Studies Center, 1988), 176.

46. Thor Heyerdahl, quoted in Kirk Holland Vestal and Arthur Wallace, *The Firm Foundation of Mormonism* (Los Angeles: LL Company, 1981), 100.

47. Norman Totten, "Categories of Evidence for Old World Contacts with Ancient America," *The Book of Mormon: The Keystone Scripture,* 190.

48. Carter, "Before Columbus," 177.

49. Ibid., 179.

50. Paul R. Cheesman, *The World of the Book of Mormon* (Bountiful, UT: Horizon Publishers, 1994), 139.

51. Carter, "Before Columbus," 170.

52. Ibid.

53. Ibid., 173.

54. Mason Inman, "Polynesians—and Their Chickens—Arrived in America Before Columbus," *National Geographic* (4 June 2007) at http://news.nationalgeographic.com/news/2007/06/070604-chickens.html (accessed 10 July 2008).

55. Cyrus Gordon, "Pre-Columbian Discoveries Link Old and New Worlds," *Ensign,* Oct. 1971, 59–60.

56. Paul R. Cheesman, "Cultural Parallels Between the Old World and the New World," *The Book of Mormon: The Keystone Scripture,* 210.

57. Carter, "Before Columbus," 182.

Book of Mormon: Other Old World Evidences

40. Angels and Books

The claim that an angel delivered a sacred record to Joseph Smith has elicited the scorn of critics and the incredulity of most of the modern world. While such an event may seem odd to modern sensibilities, like a glove it fits the world of the ancient Near East. According to one non-LDS Near Eastern expert, "Few religious ideas in the Ancient East have played a more important role than the notion of the Heavenly Tablets or the Heavenly Books [that are] handed over [to a mortal] in an interview with a heavenly being."[1]

The ancient stories typically contain the following elements: (1) A mortal receives a book from a divine being; (2) the mortal is commanded to read the book; (3) the mortal is commanded to copy the book; (4) the mortal is commanded to share the book's message with other mortals. All of these elements, of course, are found in the story of Moroni and the golden plates.

41. Jared's Ships

In the book of Ether, the Lord instructed the brother of Jared to build eight barges so the Jaredites could travel to the Americas. These barges—patterned after Noah's ark—were "tight like unto a dish," peaked at both ends, and had holes which could be "unstop[ped]" in which to allow ventilation (see Ether 2:17, 20).

When we examine non-Biblical writings that give greater details about Noah's ark than what we find in the Bible, we discover some interesting similarities to the oddities mentioned in the account of the Jaredite barges. According to some of the ancient sources, Noah's ark, when seen from the side, would have resembled a crescent moon—like the Jaredite barges, it was peaked on both ends. Depictions of actual seagoing vessels from the Tyrians and Sidonians show that some boats really had such a shape.[2]

Although the book of Ether never says that the Jaredite barges had sails, it does note (albeit casually) that the barges were driven by furious winds (Ether 6:5–9). While the Bible never mentions that wind was a factor in propelling the ark, ancient non-Biblical traditions claim that Noah's sail-less ark was driven by ferocious winds.[3]

Just as the Jaredite barges were "tight like unto a dish," these ancient documents tell us that Noah's boat had a portal that could be shut during the storm flood. The word "ark" originally meant a box—such as a chest or coffin—that was covered with a lid.[4] And just as the barges had ventilation holes, the ark had not only a door that could be shut, but at least one *nappashu*—this word is translated as "airhole" or "window" but means "breather" or "ventilator" and was not an ordinary window.[5]

The Jaredite barges took on an almost submarine-like nature, often being submerged in violent waves during their voyage. We find the exact same thing in recently rediscovered ancient documents that tell us about Noah's ark. We don't have this information in the Bible, however, and the Bible was really the only ancient source to which Joseph had access.

When the brother of Jared became concerned about the lack of light in the airtight barges, he went to the Lord and asked for some means of illumination. Glass would break the Lord replied, and they couldn't light fires, so the Lord turned the problem back over to the brother of Jared. Having complete faith in the Lord's abilities, the brother of Jared climbed a mountain and "did molten out of rock" sixteen small transparent stones. Petitioning the Lord, the brother of Jared asked Him to touch the stones so they would shine in their vessels and the Lord granted the brother of Jared his request.

Few things in the Book of Mormon have elicited more laughs from the critics than the tale of "shining stones." According to the ancient Palestine Talmud, however, the Ark was illuminated with a miraculous light-giving stone. This precious stone, the ancient documents tell us, glowed for twelve months inside the ark and would dim during the day so that Noah knew whether it was day or night. Such information was unavailable to Joseph Smith. As Dr. Nibley explains, of the four copies of the Palestine Talmud that mention the ark's shining stones, two appeared thirty years after Joseph had already translated the Book of Mormon. In 1830, when the Book of Mormon was published, there was not a single translation of the Palestine Talmud available in any modern language (even the brightest scholars had difficulty translating the Dead Sea scrolls when they were discovered in 1947 because they were written in ancient—rather than modern—Hebrew).[6]

As noted above, it was the brother of Jared, not the Lord, who suggested the idea of the shining stones. It seems reasonable to surmise that the brother of Jared was familiar with an authentic ancient tradition of Noah and his illuminated stones. One of those ancient sources (unknown in 1830) relates the tradition of a gem that could be produced by subjecting certain stones to intense heat. The resulting gem was a transparent crystal which shinned as brightly as the sun (see the same elements in Ether 3:2, 4). The common name for this gem was "Moonfriend," or *Jalakanta,* which interprets, "that which causes the waters to part." Thus the peculiar power of this shining gem enabled its possessor to pass through the depths of water unharmed. Another document tells us that the ark was also called a "bright house" and was not only a moon boat "because it was crescent-shaped and wandered through space for twelve months, but also because it was illuminated by a miraculous light."[7]

While ancient Babylonian texts tell us that the flood-boat had a "window" or *nappashu,* the "window" in Genesis comes from the Hebrew *tsohar,* which can also be translated as "shiner" or "illuminator."[8] The Book of Mormon version, which is a fuller account than any other, contains both ideas—that the barges had a ventilator as well as an illuminator.

42. Chopping Down the Execution Tree

The Gadianton Robbers were a thorn in the side of Nephite society. They attacked, raided, and murdered. In 3 Nephi 4 we read that the robbers were defeated and their leader, Zemnarihah, was finally captured and hanged for his crimes. Once he was dead, the tree upon which he was hanged was cut down—which is an interesting and unusual detail. Not surprisingly, we now know that such actions have an ancient Near Eastern precedence: "Israelite practice required that the tree upon which the culprit was hung be buried with the body. Hence the tree had to have been chopped down. Since the rabbis understood that this burial should take place immediately, the Talmud recommends hanging the culprit on a precut tree or post so that, in the words of Maimonides, 'no felling is needed.' "[9]

43. The "Rent" Garment, Part 2

In the book of Alma, we find one of the most intriguing discoveries yet. In chapter 46, Captain Moroni (not the same Moroni who led Joseph to the plates) grew angry because of the wicked Amalickiah and his followers. This group drew people away from God's Church with flattering words and sought to destroy not only the Church, but the "foundation of liberty which God had granted unto them" (v. 10). Moroni rent his coat, took a piece of it, and wrote upon it, "In memory of our God, our religion, and freedom, and our peace, our wives, and our children," (v. 12) after which he fastened it to the end of a pole. Moroni called this banner the "title of liberty."

Bowing himself down to the earth, Moroni prayed to God for the blessing of liberty for his people, after which he carried the rent garment through the streets, admonishing the people to come unto God (see Alma 46:12–20). When the people saw and heard this, they came out, rending their garments as Moroni had done, and they threw their rent garments at Moroni's feet. They did this as a sign of a covenant they were making with God. If they should fall into transgression, God could cast them at the feet of the Lamanites (their enemies) even as they had cast their garments at Moroni's feet to be trodden under foot (Alma 46:22).

When Moroni saw the people's actions, he told them that they were a remnant of Joseph "whose coat was rent by his brethren into many pieces." Then he *reminded* them of Jacob's final words to his son Joseph. Jacob saw that a part of the remnant of Joseph's coat had been preserved and had not decayed. According to Moroni, Jacob told his sons that "even as this remnant of garment of my son [Joseph] hath been preserved, so shall a remnant of the seed of my son be preserved by the hand of God, and be taken unto himself" (Alma 46:23, 24).

Genesis 37 tells the story of Joseph and his brothers, who stripped him of his garment, dipped it in goat's blood, and brought it to Jacob. They told the story that Joseph had been killed by wild beasts. While it never says that the Joseph's brothers tore his coat of many colors, Jacob thought that Joseph had been "rent in pieces" by a wild beast (v. 33).

When we compare Moroni's comments—about Joseph's coat and Jacob's vision of a surviving remnant of that coat—with other ancient non-Biblical texts, we find some interesting parallels. In the Book of Jasher for example (which was first published in English ten years after the Book of Mormon), we read that Joseph's brothers took his coat, "tore it," killed a goat, and dipped the coat in its blood, "then trampled" the coat "in the dust" before giving it back to Jacob (Jasher 43:13). Not only does the Book of Jasher mention that the coat was torn, but we also find that like the Nephites who threw their torn garments at Moroni's feet to be trodden upon, Joseph's brothers "trampled" the coat in the dirt as well.

According to the Book of Mormon—but not found in the Bible—a remnant of Joseph's coat survived. In an ancient Ethiopic manuscript known as the *Zênâhu La-Yosêf,* we read that after Joseph was sold into Egypt, Jacob would cry every day while holding Joseph's bloodstained coat. Also, according to a Muslim tradition, when Jacob sent his sons to Egypt the second time, he gave Benjamin Joseph's bloodstained coat to wear. What we find in the Book of Mormon about a remnant of Joseph's coat, correctly matches what we find in ancient Near Eastern traditions, but not recorded in the Bible.[10]

44. Hidden Records

When Moroni closed his account, adding to it the plates of Mormon, he said that he was commanded to "hide them up again in the earth" (Ether 4:3). Moroni was repeating what Book of Mormon prophets had often said before—the plates were to be buried for preservation. "Why are we so often told," writes one anti-Mormon, "that the plates were to be 'hid up unto the Lord?' This language shows the fraud which the writer designed in writing the book of Mormon."[11] Were Moroni's actions unique? They were as far as anyone knew in Joseph Smith's day. But what about our day? Are there any other similar stories of hiding sacred writ for the purpose of safe preservation, in the hopes that it would come forth in the latter days? The apocryphal Assumption of Moses gives one such example: "Moses[,] before being taken up to heaven[,] is instructed by the Lord to 'seal up' the covenant: 'Receive this writing that thou mayest know how to preserve the books which I shall deliver unto thee: and thou shalt set in order and anoint them with oil of cedar and put them away in earthen vessels in the place which he made from the beginning of the creation of the world.' "[12]

"The purpose of this hiding," notes Nibley, ". . . is to preserve the books through a '. . . period of darkness when men shall have fallen away from the true covenant and would pervert the truth.' "[13]

According to the early Christian Eusebius—who seems to be very familiar with many genuine ancient sources—we learn that Noah was commanded "to inscribe in writing the beginning, middle, and end of everything, and to bury the records in the city of Sippar."[14]

These are far from the only examples. The Nag Hammadi library and the Dead Sea Scrolls (both mentioned in the appendix) are prime examples of hidden records. We find this same theme in the rediscovered book of Enoch: "I know another mystery, that books will be given to the righteous and the wise to become a cause of joy and uprightness and much wisdom. To them will the books be given, and they will believe in them and rejoice over them, and then will all the righteous be recompensed who have learnt there from all the paths of uprightness."[15]

According to one story traced through the book of Enoch, an angel instructed the fallen Adam to take his book—the book of Adam—and hide it in the ground. In another account we find that Enoch saw Adam's book in a dream. He saw where it was buried and how he could retrieve it. The following day, he dug up the book. The characters were foreign, so Enoch interpreted them by divine revelation whereby he learned the fulness of the gospel. Non-LDS scholar C. J. Van Andel, notes Nibley, "finds it significant that the Enoch writings of the Jews are not based on the Torah but go back to unknown works of great antiquity dealing with heavenly tablets."[16]

45. Thieves and Robbers

In the Book of Mormon, we find the terms *thieves* and *robbers*. To modern Americans, the terms are interchangeable (which is what we find in the King James Version Bible). Under ancient Near Eastern law, however, there is a significant difference between the two types of criminals and how the law should punish them. A thief was typically a local person who stole from his neighbor. Thieves were tried and punished by local townspeople. A robber, however, was an outsider—a terrorist, highwayman, bandit, or guerrilla. Robbers typically belonged to organized groups that attacked towns, menaced a people, and engaged in a type of warfare. A robber was generally punished by the military and could be executed.

Among Book of Mormon villains we find bands of "robbers." The Lamanites "rob" from the Nephites but not from their own people—that would be "theft" instead of "robbery." We also read of the infamous Gadianton robbers—a band of guerillas who were outside of the Nephite society. They would attack and "rob" from the Nephites and then return to the wilderness. The Book of Mormon always uses the terms "thieves" and "robbers" correctly, according to the specific type of criminal as well as what we now know about ancient Near Eastern law.[17]

46. Nephite Money

Among supposed Book of Mormon blunders is the mention of "coins" and a monetary system. The Book of Mormon text, however, never mentions "coins." Several decades ago, the Church began to add notes, cross-references, and chapter headings. To modern readers it seemed obvious that Alma 11 was describing coins, so the chapter heading included a note that the verses in that chapter detailed a system of

"Nephite coinage." Upon closer examination, however, the text doesn't suggest that the Nephites had coins (minted coins) but they did have a monetary system, and this is what we find in the ancient New World.

Money need not take the form of coins as long as it serves as a standard measure of value. Up until recently, for instance, both the Mayan and Aztecs used cocoa beans as a form of currency.[18]

In the Book of Mormon, Alma employs a monetary system based on weight units of metal (though not coins). This was confirmed by modern science when a recent excavation in Ecuador turned up 12,000 pieces of metal money.[19] It has also been demonstrated that the Nephite monetary system was an ingenious design that was more efficient than most other ancient monetary systems.

According to Alma 11, the Nephite money system compared the value of metals and grains depending on the types and weights. As one critic has written, "One of the most amusing illustrations of our author's disposition to *beat the world* may be seen in the curious monetary scheme he devised for his remarkable people the Nephites." It is "absurd," he continues, "that these Nephites had a *fixed* standard of value for *barley*."[20] The critic is almost right. The Nephite monetary system is "curious" and "absurd" for New York State in 1830. But not for a culture derived from the ancient Near East.

The law of Mosiah, like most societies, recognized a system of legal exchange equivalents. Exchange ratios were given for gold, silver, barley, and all kinds of grain (see Alma 11:7). Likewise, in ancient Mesopotamia, the laws of Eshnunna gave an exchange equivalent of "1 kor barley for 1 shekel silver" and then establish fixed prices for "the services of harvesters, boatmen, and other workers."[21] As one scholar points out: "The primary conversion in Babylonia was between barley and silver. Nine other Babylonian provisions converted various additional commodities into silver values, followed by three more provisions that converted others into measures of barley. Thus, precious metal and grain measures were convertible into each other. The law of Mosiah featured precisely the same conversion capability: the basic measure for either gold or silver was equated with 'a measure of barley' (Alma 11:7)."[22]

In the Babylonian and Nephite economies, traders were allowed to deal with a variety of items, all convertible into silver or barley. In

Mosiah's system, for example, silver could be converted from "a measure of every kind of grain" (Alma 11:7). And like ancient Egyptian grain measurements, Mosiah's system was distinctly binary—in other words each unit of measure is half the size of the next larger unit.

Although the Nephites altered their monetary system to fit their needs, the main concept finds its roots in Near Eastern thought and was unknown in Joseph's day.

47. Sheum

Among the crops cultivated by the Nephites beginning in the second century BC we have not only barley but also sheum—for which we have no translation. Why "are there no references to [sheum] in Old World literature . . . ?" asks one critic.[23] For many years, believers had no answer. However within the last forty years, notes one LDS Scholar, "we have learned that the most important cereal grain among the Akkadians (Babylonians [& Assyrians]) of Mesopotamia was called *she'um*."[24]

Professor Hildegard Lewy, a non-Mormon specialist in ancient Babylonian languages, explains that ancient Assyrians typically applied various names to different species of grains.[25] Other scholars note that the Akkadian sheum was used "at various times to refer to barley, grains generally, and even pine nuts."[26] It's possible that the Jaredites—who originally lived in Mesopotamia—may have given the name *sheum* to some new cultivated plant they encountered in the New World. Their descendants would have continued to use this name and passed it on to future generations.

48. Land of Jerusalem

One Book of Mormon scripture that has been the frequent target of criticism is Alma 7:10, in which Alma prophesied the birth of Christ. To quote one of literally dozens of anti-Mormon writers: "The Bible declares that the Messiah of Israel was to be born in Bethlehem (Micah 5:2), and the gospel of Matthew (chapter 2, verse 1) records the fulfillment of this prophecy. But the Book of Mormon states: '. . . the son of God . . . shall be born of Mary at Jerusalem, which is the land of our forefathers.' "[27]

The irony of this accusation is that on the one hand the critics claim that Joseph Smith was an illiterate fool who didn't known where Jesus was born. On the other hand, they seem to acknowledge that Joseph knew the precise location of Jesus' baptism by John ("in Bethabara, beyond Jordan," 1 Nephi 10:9; cf. John 1:28).[28] They also seem to think he was clever enough to include in his scriptures ancient Hebrew chiastic word structures, an internal consistency of Book of Mormon geography and war campaigns, ancient traditions regarding Abraham that are not found in the Bible, a knowledge of doubled-sealed documents, and many more things that critics see as signs of Joseph's ability to *sponge* information from any source. This sponging, however, would had to have come from books in Latin, Greek, Egyptian, and Hebrew, or from writings that were not even available in the United States when he translated the Book of Mormon. Dr. William Hamblin calls this the "Idiot Savant" paradox of anti-Mormonism.[29]

Of course Joseph Smith knew that Jesus was born in Bethlehem. If Joseph was the author of the Book of Mormon, he would simply have dictated that Jesus was born in Bethlehem. That the Book of Mormon does not state this well-known fact, however, provides evidence that Joseph translated, rather than wrote, the book.

Of the several dozen Book of Mormon references to the "land of Jerusalem" and the "city of Jerusalem," we find that Joseph never uses them incorrectly. "Christ was born in a village some six miles from the city of Jerusalem," wrote Dr. Nibley, "it was not in the city, but it was in what we now know the ancients themselves designated as 'the land of Jerusalem.' Such a neat test of authenticity is not often found in ancient documents."[30]

In 1887, fifty-seven years after the publication of the Book of Mormon, new light was shed on the passage in Alma with the discovery of the Tell El Amarna Tablets. From these tablets we find that the "land of Jerusalem" was an area larger than the city itself. For instance, these tablets speak of other cities which lie in the "land of Jerusalem."[31] We find the same ancient pattern in the Book of Mormon where every major New World city is surrounded by a land of the same name.

The Dead Sea Scrolls lend additional support when it refers to Judah as the "land of Jerusalem." Non-LDS scholars have noted the following about this Dead Sea Scroll phrase: "Another interesting reference is to the 'land of Jerusalem' in Line 2 of Fragment 1. This greatly enhances the sense of historicity of the whole, since Judah or 'Yehud' (the name of the area on coins from the Persian period) by this time consisted of little more than Jerusalem and its immediate environs."[32]

The phrase "land of Jerusalem" is not in the Bible and was not current in Joseph Smith's day. It is, however, an accurate description for Jerusalem and the surrounding cities and is precisely the language that would have been used by an ancient Israelite in 600 BC—just as we find in the Book of Mormon.[33]

49. Temple Outside of Jerusalem

One of the first things which Nephi was commanded to do when he arrived in the New World was to build a temple: "And I, Nephi, did build a temple; and I did construct it after the manner of the temple of Solomon save it were not built of so many precious things; for they were not to be found upon the land, wherefore, it could not be built like unto Solomon's temple. But the manner of the construction was like unto the temple of Solomon; and the workmanship was exceedingly fine" (2 Nephi 5:16).

Just as the critics ridiculed Nephi's tale of travel through the Arabian Desert, so likewise they ridiculed the idea that the Nephites would build a temple in the New World. One states: "Nor is there so much as a hint in all the Bible that temples of any kind, except the one Temple for Israel in Jerusalem, are or were ever authorized of God to be built anywhere or at any time."[34]

Another writes: "The Nephites build on America . . . 'a temple like unto Solomon's;' . . . If the Bible be true, there could be but one temple. . . . The location for that temple was to be Jerusalem, the city of God."[35]

The Jews of Lehi's time did not believe there were never to be any other temples. At the turn of the century some papyri was found at Aswan, Egypt, and has become known as the Elephantine Papyri. The translation of the documents tells of a group of Jewish soldiers who left

Jerusalem to protect the Persian interests in South Egypt. Since the Book of Mormon contains a record of an expedition at approximately the same time, we would expect some parallels of culture and language in these two groups. As the records unfold, we find that both people are interested in building a temple soon after they arrived at their destination.[36]

50. Metal Plates and Stone Boxes

Not only does the Book of Mormon claim to have been preserved for the latter days, but it was Joseph Smith's claim that they were written on metal plates and buried in a stone box. This claim, like so many other unique claims in the Nephite scripture, has brought the scorn of the critics. The "Golden Bible," they called it. The idea of records of "gold plates" has been considered to be "preposterous" by some critics.[37] One critic who, in 1887, was "forced to reject" the Book of Mormon after a supposedly "very careful, . . . conscientious and painstaking examination of all the evidences" both "for and against it," claims that "no such records were ever engraved upon golden plates, or any other plates, in the early ages."[38]

Yet another critic writes: "It does not seem to have been pointed out to the youth [Joseph Smith] that gold will corrode if left in the earth for the number of years those plates were supposed to have been buried."[39]

Other critics have made objections concerning the brass plates that Nephi took from Laban: "This book speaks of the Jewish Scriptures, having been kept by Jews on plates of brass, six hundred years before Christ. The Jews never kept any of their records on plates of brass."[40] "The book of Mormon purports to have been originally engraved on brass plates. . . . How could brass be written on?"[41]

First, we need to understand that the Book of Mormon, like the Bible, always uses "brass" for what we know as "bronze." The term "bronze" became current after the Book of Mormon was translated."[42] Brass is an alloy of copper and zinc, whereas bronze is alloy of copper and tin. Christopher Munson points out that bronze typically contains small amounts of zinc and high-quality brass contains high amounts of zinc. Medium amounts of zinc would produce brass-like alloys that would be soft enough to inscribe, but would be more tarnish resistant than common bronze. It's therefore of interest to note that Lehi believed that the Plates of Brass would not "be dimmed any more by time" (1 Nephi 5:19).[43] So it's important to understand that the "plates of brass" were more likely plates of bronze or copper as we would understand it today. In Joseph's time, however, brass would have been a correct interpretation.

Where does this leave us with writings on metal plates? When the Dead Sea Scrolls were discovered in 1947, one of the startling finds was a copper scroll. Because writing on this metal was difficult, abbreviated and cramped scripts (which were often hard to read) were typically utilized. This recalls the Book of Mormon's claim that the record was written in "reformed Egyptian." Is this copper Dead Sea Scroll a unique example of writing on metal? In 1972 one critic explained that sixth century BC Hebrews wrote on papyrus, wood, or potsherds. He acknowledges the copper Dead Sea Scroll but argues that it was a "roll" rather than a "plate" and that it dates hundreds of years after the Lehites lived in Jerusalem.[44]

First, the critics cry that there never was any writing on metal; when some turn up, they concede that perhaps there was the rare instance of writing on metal—but not on plates. Once again, however, archaeology has come to the rescue of Joseph Smith.

Several ancient sites have yielded discoveries of bronze plates (which also have a copper base), which were used as a form of writing tablets. One plate in particular has been dated to about the same period that the Lehites fled Jerusalem with Laban's "brass" plates. A bronze plaque was discovered in 1860 near Styria, Greece, and contains laws for the distribution of land. It is now housed at the National Archaeological Museum in Athens.[45] Other metal plates have also surfaced, including a copper scroll inscribed in Hebrew and dating to the twelfth century BC. We also note the 1938 discovery of a royal proclamation liberating the Jews by "Darius the Median" that was inscribed on plates of pure gold and silver. The plates date to about Lehi's day and were buried in a carefully crafted stone box.[46]

Likewise, in 1933, a scholar discovered "two shallow, neatly made stone boxes with [sealed] lids, each containing two square plates of gold and silver."[47] Not only did ancient civilizations write on metal plates, but many of these plates were buried in stone boxes.

A twenty-page gold-leaf book found in 1926 at Old Prome was perforated so the pages could be attached together by heavy gold wire.[48] It should be remembered that the Book of Mormon plates were also held together by metal rings.

As the critics have already demonstrated, the world of Joseph Smith did not typically believe that records could be kept on metal plates. Today, however, we have hundreds of examples of ancient writings on metal plates. There is clear evidence that writings on metal plates were known in Mesopotamia during Jaredite times (from whence the Jaredites came) and we also now have evidence of metal plates, written in Semitic languages that date to the ancient Near East during Lehi's day.[49] "The discovery of writings on plates of precious metal," notes Nibley, "once the hardest thing to swallow in Joseph Smith's story, has become almost commonplace in the Near East."[50]

51. Doubled, Sealed Documents

In ancient Israel, around 600 BC (the same period that the Lehi's departed Jerusalem), Israel employed an ancient practice of using doubled, sealed, and witnessed documents. Important papyrus documents (such as legal documents) were written on a single sheet of papyri but in two parts. The text was written twice—once on the top half and once on the bottom half. The second occurrence of the text could be a duplicate copy of the original text, or it could be an abridgement of the full text. The document was folded so the abridged part was open for inspection and reading, while the second part was closed with a seal to protect it from being contaminated or altered. The sealed portion would stand as a witness or backup of the public portion.

Should concern arise that the public portion had been altered—or if clarification and extra detail was needed about any ambiguous statement in the abridged public portion—the sealed portion could be opened. Documents which were written on metal followed a similar process and the manner of sealing them was functionally the same. Two bronze tablets of the Roman emperor Trajan, for example, record an official decree in neat letters on the open side of the first bronze plate and then in a more "hurried lettering," repeated exactly the same text on the inside faces of the two plates. LDS scholar, John Welch, explains the document sealing process:

> Sealing (closing) the document was also essential, and the manner of sealing papyrus or parchment documents was relatively standard. Typically, these documents have a horizontal slit from the edge of the papyrus to the middle, between the two texts. The top half was rolled to the middle and then folded across the slit. Three holes were punched from the slit to the other side, thin papyrus bands were threaded through these holes and wrapped around the rolled-up and folded-over upper portion of the document, and on these bands the seals (wax or clay impressions) of the participants were affixed.[51]

At least three witnesses were required to verify the sealed documents and only a judge (or someone appointed by the judge) could open the sealed document. If there was a dispute about something on the open document, the judge would call forth the witnesses, open the seal, and the public text could be verified (or clarified) by what was found on the sealed portion of the text.

We are aware of this practice today thanks to archaeological discoveries, but it doesn't seem likely that Joseph could have known about this ancient practice in 1829. The Book of Mormon plates fit perfectly into the authentic ancient practice of sealed documents (see 1 Nephi 1:17; 19:1; 2 Nephi 27:10–21; 3 Nephi 5:18; Moroni 10:27), and we must remember that about two-thirds of the Book of Mormon plates were "sealed" to come forth at a later time.

52. Olive Culture

In Jacob chapter 5, Jacob quotes the ancient prophet Zenos regarding the allegory of the wild and tame olive trees and how the Israelites would be scattered and the Gentiles would eventually be grafted into the olive tree. The allegory goes into considerable detail of olive horticulture and care. What makes this all so interesting is the fact that in Joseph's day, there was no olive culture in nineteenth century New England. Is Joseph's information in Jacob 5 correct? According to a group of scholars, including Dr. William M. Hess (PhD in Plant Pathology and MS in Horticulture) and Dr. Daniel Fairbanks (PhD in Agronomy and Plant

Genetics): "Nearly all of the allegory in Jacob 5 corresponds exception-
ally well with both ancient and modern botanical principles and horticultural practices. It is hard to imagine that its author was not personally
familiar with the minute details and practices involved in raising good
olives in a Mediterranean climate."[52]

Some of many things that Zenos knew correctly about ancient olive
horticulture include:

> How to prune, dig about, dung, and nourish; how to graft tame to
> wild and wild to tame, and how to graft tame back into tame; how
> to balance tops and roots by pruning, and the reasons for doing this;
> how to save the roots of trees whose branches had decayed, and how to
> transplant branches to preserve the desired traits of good plants; how to
> preserve and store fruit and how to distinguish between good and bad
> fruit; how well plants grow on good and bad soil; how to care for trees
> to cause young and tender branches to shoot forth; that they could
> graft wild to tame to rejuvenate tame; that specific cultivars produced
> well in certain areas; . . . that they could burn an orchard to reestab-
> lish a new one; that plants grown from seeds would not have desirable
> characteristics; the importance of elimination of old wood and debris
> by burning, and how to deal with pests and pathogens; how to prevent
> heavy bearing one year and no bearing the next by proper pruning; the
> necessity to plant more than one cultivar for pollination; and how to
> propagate scions with the desirable genetic material.[53]

In three minor instances, Zenos takes metaphorical license and
makes unusual changes in horticultural techniques in order to portray
the intended meaning of the allegory. We find a similar phenomenon
in the New Testament's parable of the prodigal son. That parable begins
with the son requesting his portion of his family's inheritance while his
father was still alive. It's unlikely, however, that Jewish law in Jesus' day
would have allowed a son to acquire any inheritance while his father was
still living. The parable, however, makes this minor modification in order
to teach a point. So likewise, the allegory of the olive tree contains three
minor anomalies that are unusual from a strictly scientific point. Does
this negate the fact that the majority of the allegory relates the details of
actual ancient olive horticulture? Hardly. Our plant experts explain:

> Most of the botanical and horticultural principles in Jacob 5 are

sound and are very important for olive culture. . . . In this single chapter of the Book of Mormon there are many detailed horticultural practices and procedures that were not likely known by an untrained person, and may not have been fully appreciated by professional botanists or horticulturalists at the time the Book of Mormon was translated. Even today, outside of olive-growing areas, professional horticulturalists may not fully appreciate some of the unique aspects of olive culture. Given the extensive detail about olive culture present in Jacob 5, we must give Zenos much credit for a high degree of horticultural knowledge, which many take for granted.

Joseph Smith probably knew how to prune, dig about, dung, and nourish local fruit trees; he probably knew a little about grafting, and he may have been familiar with some other horticultural principles, but not likely those peculiarly related to olive culture.[54]

Other scholars who have studied Jacob 5 have noticed additional interesting ties to the ancient Near East. Dr. Daniel Peterson and Dr. John Gee (both experts in Near Eastern studies) have discovered that almost every detail in Jacob 5 relating to olive culture "can be confirmed in four classical authors whose authority on the subject can be traced back to Syro-Palestine" (the culture from whence the Lehites emerged).

Zenos's parable fits into the pattern of ancient olive cultivation remarkably well. The placing of the villa above the vineyards means that, when the master gives instructions to his servants, they have to "go down" into the vineyard (Jacob 5:15, 29, 38). It was also customary for the master of the vineyard to have several servants (cf. Jacob 5:7, 10–11, 15–16, 20–21, 25–30, 33–35, 38, 41, 48–50, 57, 61–62, 70–72, 75). When only one servant is mentioned in Zenos's parable, the reference is most likely to the chief steward. Likewise, Zenos's mention of planting (Jacob 5:23–25, 52, 54), pruning (Jacob 5:11, 47, 76; 6:2), grafting (Jacob 5:8,9–10,17–18, 30, 34, 52, 54–57, 60, 63–65, 67–68), digging (Jacob 5:4, 27, 63–64), nourishing (Jacob 5:4, 12, 27, 28, 58, 71; 6:2), and dunging (Jacob 5:47, 64, 76), as well as the fact that dunging occurs less frequently in the parable than the nourishing, all mark it as an authentic ancient work. The unexpected change of wild olive branches to tame ones (Jacob 5:17–18) would have seemed a divine portent to our ancient authorities.[55]

If Joseph had borrowed the information from these classical authors, then he would have read all four authors' works (since each author only gives part of the details), and he would have known Latin and Greek in 1829 since most of the works were not available in English until the twentieth century. It must also be remembered that Joseph was dictating the Book of Mormon at a rate of about eight pages a day; he had no notes or books in front of him from which to cull information; he didn't revise the original manuscript to ensure that the olive horticulture was accurate; and in all probability, neither he nor anyone in his vicinity had ever experienced olive horticulture. What are the chances of him getting such things right?

53. King Benjamin's Speech

Nearly four hundred and fifty years after Lehi and his family landed in the Americas, there arose a king among the people by the name of Benjamin. King Benjamin, a righteous man, established peace in the land. In the book of Mosiah (Mosiah was a righteous son of the king), we read how in about 124 BC, the king sent a proclamation, "unto all the people who were in the land of Zarahemla that thereby they might gather themselves together, to go up to the temple to hear the words which his father [Benjamin] should speak unto them" (Mosiah 1:18).

The Nephites gathered at the temple to hear King Benjamin speak. Many families traveled for miles and pitched their tents near the temple. So many people arrived that there was not enough room within the temple walls to hold them all. King Benjamin ordered that a tower be built, upon which he could stand to teach the people. The words of King Benjamin's speech were written down and passed on to those who were unable to come and hear Benjamin's speech (see Mosiah 2:1–2, 5, 7–8).

Secondary to the spiritual insight gained by reading the sermon of King Benjamin, we also find additional evidence of the Book of Mormon's link with the ancient Old World. "There can be no doubt at all," writes Nibley, "that in the Book of Mosiah we have a long and complete description of a typical national assembly in the antique pattern. . . . There is no better description of the event in any single ritual text than is found in the Book of Mosiah."[56]

Modern research suggests that King Benjamin's speech fits the patterns of ancient "farewell addresses." Non-Mormon scholar William S. Kurz published a detailed study identifying twenty elements which are common to biblical farewell addresses in general. Kurz explains that no single speech contains all of these elements and some contain more than others. Moses's farewell speech, for example, contains sixteen of these elements, while Paul's farewell address contains fourteen. When we use Kurz's criteria, we find that King Benjamin's speech contains at least sixteen direct elements and others are implied.[57]

Not only does King Benjamin's speech have strong similarities to ancient Near Eastern traditions, but so does Mosiah's coronation. After years of research, scholars now recognize that Israelite coronations had distinct elements and patterns. All of them match the coronation of Benjamin's son, Mosiah. Nibley observes, "Imagine a twenty-three-year old backwoodsman [Joseph Smith] in 1829 giving his version of what an ancient coronation ceremony would be like—what would be done and said, how, and by whom? Put the question to any college senior or dean of humanities today and see what you get."[58]

Nibley shows that the Book of Mormon fits perfectly into the pattern of the Eastern coronation rite, including the building of a tower before the king's speech, the type of speech, the blessings pronounced on the people, and several other points of similarities that are too close to dismiss as lucky guesses. In addition, recently gathered research indicates that even the timing and gathering of Benjamin's speech fits Old World patterns.

Today, many scholars recognize that the three Jewish fall festivals—Rosh Hashanah (New Year), Yom Kippur (Day of Atonement), and Sukkot (Feast of Tabernacles)—originally developed from an earlier single festival. This is exactly what we find in King Benjamin's address in the Book of Mormon. During Lehi's day there would have been only one festival, incorporating all three themes, rather than three different festivals. The themes contained in Benjamin's speech parallel, with amazing accuracy, the characteristics of what scholars now know of the ancient Israelite festival, including the falling down before God, the stress on the Atonement, and the people living in tents to listen to the king's speech.[59]

54. Disarming Ammon

In Alma 17 we read how Ammon protected King Lamoni's flocks from a group of Lamanites. A battle ensued wherein Ammon killed several of the Lamanites and then "smote off" the arms of the cadavers and brought the arms back to King Lamoni (Alma 17:37–39). While we might not have been surprised had Alma brought the heads of the Lamanites to the king, it sounds odd to Americans who read that Ammon brought the arms of his enemies to the king.

When we examine ancient Near Eastern customs, however, the strangeness finds a home. At least as early as the ninth century BC, artwork in the ancient Near East attests to the practice of cutting off the arms, hands, feet, or other body parts of vanquished enemies. Scholars who have studied this ancient custom suggest the severed limbs might have served as vouchers for rewards or mercenary pay upon presentation to an authority.[60]

It has just recently been shown that the Aztecs had a similar practice. Ancient artwork depicts Aztec warriors holding the severed arms of their enemies like trophies. According to a review of one early Spanish conquistador's writings, when Spaniard soldiers were captured by the Aztecs, the warriors would cut off their victims' arms, and then the Aztecs would taunt those Spanish soldiers who were still within earshot.

Aztecs who proved their prowess in battle often gained social privileges such as the right to wear special clothing and to enjoy special foods. Bringing back the severed arms of an enemy was a one way to prove valor in combat.[61]

55. Columbus

In the early part of the Book of Mormon, Nephi saw in vision a "man among the Gentiles" who left his people and crossed "many waters" (1 Nephi 13:12). Nephi saw that "the Spirit of God" was with this man who eventually came to the Americans and the descendants of the Lehites. Latter-day Saints have interpreted this verse as referring to Christopher Columbus.

Critics have charged that this was an easy prophesy to make for someone like Joseph Smith, who already knew that Columbus had sailed to the Americas. In last few decades, however, there has been a growth in scholarship regarding Columbus—much of it starting in 1991 with the translation and publication of Columbus's *Libro de las profecias.* This new look at Columbus reveals a spiritual man who was driven, in part, with a desire to spread Christianity. Among his favorite scriptural passages was John 10:16 which quotes Christ stating that "other sheep I have which are not of this fold" and the Savior's desire to bring them all together so there would "be one fold, and one shepherd." Columbus believed that he was guided to the New World by the Holy Spirit. He wrote: "With a hand that could be felt, the Lord opened my mind to the fact that it would be possible to sail from here to the Indies, and he opened my will to desire to accomplish the project. This was the fire that burned within me. . . . Who can doubt that this fire was not merely mine, but also of the Holy Spirit who encouraged me with a radiance of marvelous illumination from his sacred Holy Scriptures, by a most clear and powerful testimony . . . urging me to press forward?"[62]

Later in life, after he had made his journey to the New World, he said that the Lord had made him a "messenger of the new heaven and the new earth . . . and he showed me the place where to find it."[63]

Notes

1. Brent E. McNeely, "The Book of Mormon and the Heavenly Motif," *Reexploring the Book of Mormon,* 26.
2. Nibley, *An Approach to the Book of Mormon,* 279.
3. Ibid., 280–81; Nibley, *Lehi in the Desert,* 180–81.
4. Nibley, *An Approach to the Book of Mormon,* 279.
5. Ibid.
6. Ibid., 283–84.
7. Ibid., 285–86, 289.
8. Nibley, *Lehi in the Desert,* 364.
9. John W. Welch, "The Execution of Zemnarihah," Reexploring the Book of Mormon, 250–251.
10. John Tvedtnes, "Ancient Texts in Support of the Book of Mormon," Echoes and Evidences of the Book of Mormon, eds., Donald W. Parry,

Daniel C. Peterson, and John W. Welch (Provo: FARMS, 2002), 236–38.

11. Sunderland, *Mormonism Exposed and Refuted,* 46.

12. Nibley, *An Approach to the Book of Mormon,* 137.

13. Ibid.

14. Nibley, "New Approaches to Book of Mormon Study," *The Prophetic Book of Mormon,* 75.

15. Quoted in Vernon W Mattson, Jr., *The Dead Sea Scrolls and Other Important Discoveries* (Salt Lake City, UT: Buried Record Productions, 1979), 27.

16. Hugh Nibley, "A Strange Thing in the Land: The Return of the Book of Enoch," *Enoch the Prophet* (Salt Lake City, UT: Deseret Book; Provo, UT: FARMS, 1986), 145.

17. John W. Welch, "Thieves and Robbers," *Reexploring the Book of Mormon,* 248–49.

18. Piedad Peniche Rivero, "When Cocoa was used as Currency—pre-Columbian America—The Fortunes of Money," (January 1990) at http://findarticles.com/p/articles/mi_m1310/is_1990_Jan/ai_8560999 (accessed 7 July 2008); Virginia Morell, "The Lost Language of Coba," *Science 86,* March 1986, 52.

19. John L. Sorenson, *An Ancient American Setting for the Book of Mormon* (Salt Lake City, UT: Deseret Book; Provo, UT: FARMS, 1985), 233.

20. Lamb, *The Golden Bible,* 302–303.

21. John W. Welch, "The Law of Mosiah," *Reexploring the Book of Mormon,* 160.

22. John W. Welch, "A Steady Stream of Significant Recognitions," *Echoes and Evidences of the Book of Mormon,* 349.

23. Key, *A Biologist Examines the Book of Mormon,* 1.

24. John L. Sorenson, "How Could Joseph Smith Write So Accurately about Ancient American Civilizations?" *Echoes and Evidences of the Book of Mormon,* 288.

25. Robert R. Bennett, "Barely and Wheat in the Book of Mormon," at http://farms-stage.byu.edu/publications/transcripts/?id=126 (accessed 4 July 2008).

26. Ibid.

27. Walter Martin, *The Kingdom of the Cults* (Minneapolis: Bethany Fellowship Inc., 1977), 166–67.

28. Daniel C. Peterson, "On Alma 7:10 and the Birthplace of Jesus

Christ," at http://farms.byu.edu/display-print.php?table=transcripts &id=37 (accessed 3 August 2008).

29. William J. Hamblin, "Basic Methodological Problems with the Anti-Mormon Approach to the Geography and Archaeology of the Book of Mormon," *Journal of Book of Mormon Studies* 2, no.1 (1993): 173.

30. Nibley, *An Approach to the Book of Mormon,* 81–82.

31. Ibid.; Nibley, *Lehi in the Desert,* 6–7.

32. "Insights: An Ancient Window," FARMS (1994) at http://farms-stage. byu.edu/publications/insights/?vol=14&num=3&id=29 (accessed 4 July 2008).

33. Gordon C. Thomasson, "Revisiting the Land of Jerusalem," *Pressing Forward with the Book of Mormon,* 14–141.

34. Decker and Hunt, *Godmakers,* 209.

35. Hyde, *Mormonism: Its Leaders and Designs,* 229.

36. Paul R. Cheesman, *Ancient Writing on Metal Plates: Archaeological Findings Support Mormon Claims* (Bountiful, UT: Horizon, 1985), 36.

37. Nibley, *An Approach to the Book of Mormon,* 17.

38. Lamb, *The Golden Bible,* 11.

39. Stuart Martin, *The Mystery of Mormonism* (London: Odhams Press Lmtd., 1920), 27.

40. Sunderland, *Mormonism Exposed and Refuted,* 46.

41. Ibid., 44.

42. Nibley, *An Approach to the Book of Mormon,* 88.

43. FARMS Newsletter Oct. 1983, 3; see also Jeffrey R. Chadwick, "Lehi's House at Jerusalem and the Land of His Inheritance," *Glimpses of Lehi's Jerusalem,* eds., John W. Welch, David Rolph Seely, and JoAnn H. Seely (Provo, UT: FARMS, 2004), 114–15.

44. Anthony A. Hoekema, *The Four Major Cults* (Grand Rapids: William B. Erdmans Publishing Co., 1963), 82–83.

45. Diane E. Wirth, *A Challenge to the Critics* (Bountiful, UT: Horizon Publishers, 1986), 41–42.

46. Nibley, *An Approach to the Book of Mormon,* 18–19.

47. H. Curtis Wright, "Ancient Burials of Metal Documents in Stone Boxes," *Journal of Library History* 16, no. 1 (Winter 1981): 49.

48. Cheesman, *Ancient Writings on Metal Plates,* 86.

49. Ibid., 69, 82.

50. Nibley, "New Approaches to the Book of Mormon," *The Prophetic Book of Mormon,* 76.

51. Welch, "A Steady Stream of Significant Recongitions," 377.

52. Wilford M. Hess, Daniel J. Fairbanks, John W. Welch, and Jonathan K. Driggs, "Botanical Aspects of Olive Culture Relevant to Jacob 5," *The Allegory of the Olive Tree,* eds., Stephen Dr. Ricks and John W. Welch (Salt Lake City, UT: Deseret Book; Provo: FARMS, 1994), 505.

53. Ibid., 552–53.

54. Ibid., 552, 554.

55. John Gee and Daniel C. Peterson, "Graft and Corruption: On Olives and Olive Culture in the Pre-Modern Mediterranean," *The Allegory of the Olive Tree,* 223–24.

56. Nibley, *An Approach to the Book of Mormon,* 255–56.

57. John W. Welch and Daryl R. Hague, "Benjamin's Sermon as a Traditional Ancient Farewell Address," *King Benjamin's Speech: "That Ye May Learn Wisdom,* eds., John W. Welch and Stephen D. Ricks (Provo, UT: FARMS, 1998), 89–95, 104–105.

58. Nibley, *Since Cumorah,* 279.

59. John A. Tvedtnes, "King Benjamin and the Feast of Tabernacles," *By Study and Also by Faith,* 2 vols., eds., John M. Lundquist and Stephen D. Ricks (Salt Lake City, UT: Deseret Book; Provo: FARMS, 1990) 2:197–237.

60. John M. Lundquist and John W. Welch, "Ammon and Cutting Off the Arms of Enemies," *Reexploring the Book of Mormon,* 180–81.

61. Bruce H. Yerman, "Ammon and the Mesoamerican Custom of Smiting Off Arms," *Journal of Book of Mormon Studies* (1999) 18:1, 46–47.

62. Quoted in Daniel C. Peterson, "Not Joseph's and Not Modern," *Echoes and Evidences of the Book of Mormon,* 201.

63. Ibid., 203.

Book of Mormon: New World Evidences

56. *Book of Mormon Geography*

Is there an official Church position on the location of Book of Mormon events? The answer is a simple no. Harold B. Lee once advised the Saints not to become too concerned with Book of Mormon geography: "Some say the Hill Cumorah was in southern Mexico (and someone pushed it down still farther) and not in western New York. Well, if the Lord wanted us to know where it was or where Zarahemla was, he'd have given us latitude and longitude, don't you think?"[1]

Despite what members may assume, just because Joseph Smith spoke with Moroni and translated the Book of Mormon, doesn't mean that he necessarily knew where the events took place. Joseph never claimed to have received revelation on the question of Book of Mormon geography, and some of his comments imply that he was open to suggestions.

Most members have believed (and perhaps still believe) that Book of Mormon events took place over the entire hemisphere of North and South America. A cursory reading of the Book of Mormon suggests that North America was the land northward and that South America was the land southward. Present-day Panama naturally appears to be the "narrow neck" of land connecting the north and the south.

It is very possible that Joseph Smith, most of his contemporaries, and probably most modern-day prophets assumed and even embraced this hemispheric view. Without revelation to settle the issue, Joseph was as free to speculate as anyone else. The truth is, however, that the textual evidence within the Book of Mormon itself tells us that a hemispheric geography is untenable. The fact that Joseph could have made incorrect assumptions about the geography of events in his own book supports the proposition that Joseph was not the author, but was instead, the translator.

The decisive factor supporting a limited geography is travel distance between extreme ends of Book of Mormon cities. Where noted, travel distances are always mentioned in terms of how long the trip took. All such trips are short, indicating very limited scale of possibly no more than a few hundred miles—perhaps a total area about the size of Tennessee. While such a small area may seem unusual to modern readers, it should be noted that 95 percent of the Old Testament took place in an area only 150 miles long and fewer than 75 miles wide.

While there are several theories as to the precise location of this limited Book of Mormon geography, the virtual consensus among the most learned LDS scholars puts the events in Mesoamerica—with the Isthmus of Tehuantepec as the narrow neck of land. There are several supporting evidences for a Mesoamerican theory. These evidences match what we find in the Book of Mormon and, not surprisingly, were unknown or virtually unknown to early nineteenth-century farmers in upstate New York.

- **Writings.** Mesoamerica is the only place (so far discovered) that had a sophisticated writing system during Book of Mormon times.
- **Advanced cities and fortifications.** Thanks to archaeology we now know that such cities and fortifications existed in Mesoamerica during Book of Mormon times.
- **Rivers.** Rivers must match in size and in portion of what we find in the Nephite scripture. Such correlations are found in Mesoamerica.
- **Climate.** The Book of Mormon never mentions snow or cold in a New World setting and suggests a temperate climate for growing such things as "barley."
- **Culture.** Both Book of Mormon cultures and Mesoamerican cultures had developed agriculture and commerce.
- **Volcanism.** The destruction described in 3 Nephi following the

New World appearance of Christ, is best explained by volcanic activity and earthquakes. Mesoamerica lies in a hot zone of frequent earthquakes and volcanic activity.

The vast majority of LDS archaeologists, anthropologists, and New World experts believe that Mesoamerica meets the requirements for lands described in the Book of Mormon. Book of Mormon geography is, first of all, internally consistent—it provides over seven hundred geographic references and never trips up in explaining directions of travel and geographic locations.[2] Second, such a consistent geography can't just be dropped in any location in the world; it must not only fit the six criteria mentioned above (which accurately match what we know about ancient Mesoamerica), but geographically it must also match hundreds of mutually dependant variables including hills, rivers, seas, and so forth. As John Clark, the director of the New World Archaeological Foundation explains, rather than counting a credible Book of Mormon geography as single evidence for the book's authenticity, "it actually counts for several hundred. The probability of [Joseph] guessing reams of details all correctly is zero."[3]

Third, a New World geography must correctly account for the population figures that we find in the Book of Mormon (which mentions the existence of millions of people). As Dr. Clark observes, "Mesoamerica is the only area in the Americas that sustained the high population densities mentioned in the Book of Mormon, and for the times specified."[4] That such correlations are genuine to real experts in Mesoamerica is seen in the following story of two Mesoamerican archaeologists, Dr. Kim Goldsmith and her husband, Alejandro Sarabia, who converted to the Church:

> Long before becoming Mormons, they both had earned degrees in archaeology and for several decades had been engaged in research at Teotihuacan—the largest archaeological zone in all of Mesoamerica and a site that flourished from about 150 BC to AD 750 (which is partially contemporary with Book of Mormon times). Alejandro is currently the Site Director at Teotihuacan. While Kim and Alejandro were converted through a spiritual witness, they believe that the Book of Mormon is an authentic ancient text and that it has an overwhelming number of important points that easily fit in with myriad geographic and cultural traits of ancient Mesoamerica.[5]

57. Unknown New World

Despite the fact that we have seen great strides in Mesoamerican studies, scientists still know relatively little about Book of Mormon lands during Book of Mormon times. Dr. Nibley quotes A.A. Anguiano, who wrote in 1967 that from the years of Pre-Classical occupation of Mesoamerica (which would have been the Book of Mormon era), "not a single item of clothing has been found."[6] According to researchers in 1980, less that 1 percent of all known ancient Mesoamerican sites had been excavated, and of that 1 percent, only a very small amount of have anything to do with remains from Book of Mormon times.[7]

There are several reasons why knowledge of ancient Mesoamerica is somewhat limited. The harsh jungle terrain is just part of the problem. Money, or rather the lack of money, is a major problem in locating, researching, and excavating archaeological sites. Many known sites have not been excavated by professional archaeologists because of the lack of funds. A third serious problem, as noted by *National Geographic,* is the looting of archaeological sites before professionals have had a chance to study them: "Looting still occurs frequently enough to deprive us of priceless knowledge of the fascinating ancient Maya civilization. . . . In their efforts to slice beautiful stone carvings into portable, marketable segments, looters have totally destroyed many precious hieroglyphic inscriptions."[8]

A fourth problem lies in the fact that many modern cities are built over archaeological remains. This practice is not of wholly modern nature for it has been discovered that quite often Mesoamerican cities were built upon other older Mesoamerican cities. Palenque, for instance, which was built by the Mayans after 600 AD, was also inhabited during Book of Mormon times. "Ruin after ruin among the Mayas has now been found to be built on top of earlier structures that *do* date to Book of Mormon times."[9]

While Mesoamerican archaeology has seen tremendous advances in the last two decades, a lot more research, money, and time will be required before a full picture and evaluation of ancient Mesoamerican life can be made. The emerging picture, however, fits neatly into the descriptions contained within the pages of the Book of Mormon. What little knowledge we do have about the ancient New World has come to light in very recent years. In the days of Joseph Smith, almost nothing was known about the former inhabitants of Mesoamerica. A professional anthropologist, Dr. John Sorenson explains: "Joseph Smith could not have known in 1830 from published books or his contemporaries that an ancient civilization had existed anywhere in the Americas. To all settlers of the western New York frontier, an 'Indian' was just a savage."[10]

One recent study examined what authentic pre-400 AD Mesoamerican history would have been available to Joseph Smith in western New York in 1829 when he translated the Book of Mormon. The study demonstrates that the only authoritative sources available on Mesoamerica during Joseph's day dealt almost exclusively with cultures that existed after Book of Mormon times. It was only after the Book of Mormon was published that works began to come forth dealing with the pre-400 AD cultures of Mesoamerica.[11] The first real knowledge of ancient Mesoamerica came to light in the 1840s when, as noted in the magazine *Archaeology*, "John Lloyd Stephens . . . first brought the spectacular ruins of ancient Maya civilization to the attention of American readers."[12]

Over three hundred years before Stephens made his journey to Mesoamerica, the Spanish had lived among the natives, viewed their customs, and wrote manuscripts containing information of the ancient inhabitants of the New World. Three centuries later, after searching written histories which he needed to understand his discoveries, Stephens complained that none of these manuscripts were available even to a man of his stature.[13] If these early Spanish and Mesoamerican documents were unavailable to John L. Stephens in 1840, they most surely were unavailable to the young Prophet, Joseph Smith. The world of the early Americans was unknown to both Joseph Smith and the most learned men of his time.

58. Mesoamerican Cultures

"There is no correspondence whatever," wrote one critic in 1965, "between archaeological sites and cultures as revealed by scientific investigations, and as recorded in the *Book of Mormon*."[14] That was likely true when he penned those words. Today, however, when we compare Book of Mormon cultural history with what is known of Mesoamerican

MICHAEL R. ASH

history for the same period, we find some amazing similarities, and no areas of serious conflict. Sorenson illustrates, for instance, that in Mesoamerican sites that are likely candidates for Nephite cities, there is an absence of monumental religious art and idol worship. In areas which were most likely Lamanite cities (according to geographical studies), religious decadence, idol worship, and paganism were prevalent.[15]

Sorenson has shown that enough significant things are shared in common with the contents of the Book of Mormon and Mesoamerican cultural traits, that serious additional investigation is warranted. Included among this list of common cultural traits are:

> The cosmos was considered to be formed in layered fashion with multiple realms above, the earth's surface between, and one or more underworlds [see Alma 1:15]; . . . caves and water holes connected with the lower world [1 Nephi 12:16]. . . . In legendary times a catastrophic flood took place which destroyed all but a handful of people [Alma 10:22; 3 Nephi 22:9; Ether 6:7]. . . . Mountains were holy places, the home of a god or gods, whose name(s) often included the term mountain [2 Nephi 18:18; Ether 3:1; 4:1]. . . . Either real hills or mountains or artificial elevations were contact points where men communicated with deity, made offerings, received visitations, erected a dwelling for him, buried the dead, etc. Ascending such a mountain or mound symbolized ascent to heaven [1 Nephi 11:1; 17:7; 2 Nephi 4:25; 24:13; Alma 1: 15; 31:13–23].[16]

Modern archaeology also verifies that the level of civilization depicted in the Book of Mormon generally agrees with Nephite and Lamanite chronology. The peak of Book of Mormon civilization, for instance, was from the first century BC to the AD fourth century. Before AD 100, the civilizations were small in numbers, and after 100 BC, we see a growth in cultural, political, and economic aspects of an expanding society. By the third and fourth centuries AD, both the Nephites and Lamanites had built cities and impressive public buildings (4 Nephi 1), and were engaging in trade and large-scale war (Mormon 1–6).[17] When we compare this picture to what we find in Mesoamerican archaeology and historical research, the similarities are impressive and fit the Book of Mormon in ways that Joseph Smith could not have known.

In addition to the archaeological support of large civilizations—in the right places and in the right times—we have some other interesting parallels between Mesoamerica and the Book of Mormon. In Alma 63:5–6, for example, we read that just before the time of Christ, Hagoth built ships near the west sea by the narrow neck of the land and sent explorers northward. In no other Book of Mormon passage do we read of New World shipbuilding and exploring by sea. On the west coast (Pacific) side of the Isthmus of Tehuantepec (the area that most LDS scholars have identified as the "narrow neck of land" for many decades) are a pair of large lagoons that would have been ideal for shipbuilding and launching of water vessels. Mesoamericanists now agree that the native inhabitants built seagoing rafts and traveled from the Isthmus of Tehuantepec both northward and southward in trading expeditions.[18]

Near the end of the Book of Mormon, we read the people had become so depraved that some practiced ceremonial human sacrifice (Mormon 4:11–15, 21) and cannibalism (Moroni 9:8–10). "Evidence for these heinous practices at about the same period of time," notes Dr. Sorenson, "have been revealed by archaeological excavations, but not until a long time after the Book of Mormon translation was published."[19]

59. The Marketplace

In Helaman 7:10 we read that Nephi went to pray on a tower in a garden by "the highway which led to the chief market." This is the only use of the word "market" in the entire Book of Mormon and it is mentioned only in passing. One researcher notes: "One hardly notices the words *chief market* in this particular chapter, and upon deeper perusal of the verse, the use of the two words at first seems unnecessary. Why add this description? If Joseph Smith were authoring the book, there would be no need to include such a description. In fact, any unusual word or description could jeopardize the integrity of the work. After all, the native Americans with whom he was familiar had no marketplaces!"[20]

The verse suggests, however, that if there were a chief market, then there had to be other markets in the city. Turning to Mesoamerica we find that a marketplace did indeed exist in ancient Mesoamerican times. Such markets would have been open-air and generally located in the main plaza or courtyards near the temples (today they are located near churches). Not only did large Mesoamerican cities have markets, but they typically had a main or chief market. Non-LDS scholars have made several comments about the chief market and its importance as an economic institution. Archaeological digs also support the existence of—what non-LDS scholars refer to as—"a central market" and "the central marketplace."[21]

60. New World Writings

One reason that LDS scholars believe Book of Mormon events transpired in Mesoamerica is it's the only place in the western hemisphere where a true writing system can be found for the Book of Mormon period. Since Joseph Smith's day, however, the critics have argued that there were no complex writing systems known in the New World during Book of Mormon times. As recently as 1985, one critic wrote: "The Book of Mormon was supposedly written during the period in question [between 600 BC and AD 400], but there is no evidence that Indians had anything other than simple pictorial writing at that time. They wrote no books."[22]

This critic is simply voicing an argument that has been leveled at the Book of Mormon since it first came from the press. That argument, however, can no longer stand up in the face of archaeological finds.

First, we wish to point out that literacy among the ancient New World inhabitants would not have been widespread. Dr. Sorenson explains that "in archaic civilizations like those of Egypt or the Nephites in America, most people were not literate."[23] This is the same thing we find in ancient Mesoamerica. A sophisticated writing system was known, however, both to certain Book of Mormon peoples as well as the ancient inhabitants of Mesoamerica. It is likely that this writing system was limited to the civic officials or the priestly class. This is exactly what we find in the Book of Mormon where we read that each person chosen to add to the records was taught their unique "reformed Egyptian" script. As the Nephites fell into apostasy, and new governments usurped old governments, the knowledge of this secret, or unique, script was lost.

Just because the Book of Mormon came to a close, however, does not mean that writing in the New World ceased. Others could have kept records, but their perspectives would have been different than the one recorded by Nephite prophets. These new or different (possibly even contemporary) records may share certain aspects with the Book of Mormon, but none would contain material quite like the Nephite scripture. Likewise, Sorenson points out that "thousands of documents from the ancient Mediterranean and Near Eastern area shared much of the form but little of the substance of the scriptures we know as the Bible."[24]

For years, the critics have claimed that the ancient Americans did not have a complex writing system, and certainly did not write books. Science has changed all that. Excavation of a tomb in Mirador uncovered the "remnants of two ancient bark paper books or codices."[25] An article in *Science 86* explains that the Maya "wrote books on folded bark concerning historical, mythological, religious, astronomical, and mathematical matters (only four of these books have survived)."[26]

Why have only four out of hundreds of Mesoamerican codices (books) survived? Part of the reason, of course, would be deterioration with time. A second reason was that the Spanish destroyed these written records. In July, 1562, Bishop Fray Diego de Landa, of Yucatan, ordered the destruction of a priceless collection of Mayan codices because he claimed that they contained the "superstitions and lies of the devil."[27] Landa wrote: "These people (of Yucatan) also made use of certain characters or letters, with which they wrote in their books their ancient affairs and their sciences, and with these and drawings and with certain signs in their drawings, they understood their affairs and made others understand them and taught them. We found a great number of characters in these books . . . we burned them all, which they regretted to an amazing degree and caused them affliction."[28]

The Spanish priests, in their zeal to wipe out what they believed to be pagan superstitions, destroyed hundreds of books which might have shed light on the ancient inhabitants of the Americas.

61. *"It Came to Pass," Part 2*
We noted earlier (section 15) that "and it came to pass" and similar phrases (as found in the Book of Mormon) are authentic ancient

Old World phrases that were necessary for transition in Hebrew and Egyptian scripts. When we turn to the New World we find some interesting parallels as well. Recently translated Mayan glyphic writings demonstrate that the Ancient Americans had two common glyphs that were used to transition a text. These two glyphs have been translated by non-Mormon scholars as, "and it came to pass," and "and now" or "and thus."[29] All three transitional phrases are also frequently found in the Nephite record.

62. Tumbaga

According to Joseph Smith, the Book of Mormon was "engraven on plates which had the appearance of gold, each plate was six inches wide and eight inches long and not quite so thick as common tin. . . . The volume was something near six inches in thickness."[30]

For years the critics have claimed that there could not have been any "golden plates" because the plates would have been too heavy for Joseph to carry: "this mass of gold plates, as they were not so compactly pressed as boxed tin, would have weighed nearly 200 lbs."[31] And "if the plates were gold plates of the dimensions indicated they must have weighed between 175 and 225 pounds."[32]

Those who handled the Book of Mormon, however, claim that the plates were much lighter: "William Smith, a brother of the Prophet who had handled and hefted the plates in a pillowcase, claimed on several occasions that the set of plates weighed about sixty pounds . . . , as did Willard Chase . . . , while Martin Harris said that they weighed forty to fifty pounds."[33]

How do we account for the discrepancy? First, the critics are wrong in their estimations. Researcher Read Putnam explains that according to the approximate measurements of the plates as given by Joseph Smith—6 in. x 8 in. x 6 in.—the Book of Mormon plates would equal a volume of about 288 cubic inches: "A solid block of gold of totaling 288 cubic inches would weigh a little over 200 pounds. . . . But plates would weigh much less than a solid block of the same metal. The unevenness left by the hammering and air spaces between the separate plates would reduce the weight to probably less than 50 percent of the solid block."[34]

One hundred pounds, however, is still much heavier than the sixty or so pounds suggested by several Book of Mormon witnesses. The weight question, I find, is a strong vindication for the book's authenticity. If Joseph Smith was the brilliant con man that the critics have made him out to be, he would surely have known that golden plates, in the dimensions he described, would have weighed at least one hundred pounds. If Joseph was making up the whole story, he would have given different dimensions. He could have described the record in any manner he chose. Joseph could have claimed that the record was written on parchment, bark, stone, or on a scroll. If he had claimed that the Book of Mormon had been preserved on a scroll by descendants of Jews who had inhabited the New World, his story might have sounded even more believable to the people of his day. Everyone knew that the ancient Jews wrote on scrolls.

Instead, however, Joseph Smith claimed (and was ridiculed by the learned) that the record had been preserved on metal plates. If he had been making all this up, he could have chosen any metal he desired. Obviously gold is the most attractive. Joseph could have said that the plates were made of pure gold and given smaller dimensions to accommodate a lighter weight. Joseph, however, gave the dimensions which he saw and the witnesses gave the approximate weights which they hefted. Joseph may have understood that "gold" plates of those dimensions would have weighed at least one hundred pounds and thus he described the plates as having the "appearance of gold." Turning then to the New World, we find that the ancient inhabitants did indeed make engravings upon a metal which was lighter than gold but had the "appearance of gold."

In 1984, Heather Lechtman, writing for *Scientific America*, addressed the recent discovery of several large metal objects in South America. Most of these objects were made out of hammered sheet copper. When these copper sheets were first unearthed, they were covered with a green corrosion. Once the corrosion was removed, however, they discovered that the copper had originally been covered with a thin layer of silver or gold so that these sheets "appeared to be made entirely out of those precious metals."[35] Lechtman explains that the most important alloy discovered at these South American sites was a mixture of copper and gold known as "tumbaga." When copper and gold (the only two colored metals known to man) are melted together, they mix and stay mixed after they cool and solidify. This alloy was known not only in South America but in Mesoamerica as well.[36]

Tumbaga ranged from 97 percent gold to 97 percent copper with traces of up to 18 percent of other metals, impurities, or silver. Once the gold finish was applied to the tumbaga, it would appear to be made of solid gold. In light of this evidence, it may be significant to note that Joseph's younger brother William (who probably never handled the plates himself but would have heard the testimony of two brothers and a father who had handled the plates) said that the Nephite record was "a mixture of gold and copper."[37]

Putnam explains that tumbaga, "the magic metal, can be cast, drawn, hammered, gilded, soldered, welded, plated, hardened, annealed, polished, engraved, embossed, and inlaid."[38] Tumbaga will destroy itself, however, if it is not stored properly. It is therefore interesting to note that the Book of Mormon plates were laid atop two stones which lay across the bottom of the stone box so that the plates would not be exposed to water or dirt.

Too little gold in the Book of Mormon plates would have made them brittle, and too much gold would have made them too heavy as well as increasing the danger of distortion during engraving. Thus, according to Putnam's calculations, the Book of Mormon plates were probably between 8 and 12 carat gold and would have weighed between 53 and 86 pounds. To the eye, however, the tumbaga plates would have had the appearance of pure gold.[39] Researchers from FARMS explain:

> If the plates were made of the tumbaga alloy, other details fit into place. Take the color of the plates: The plates are consistently described as "gold" and "golden." When tumbaga (which is red) is treated with any simple acid (citric acid will do), the copper in the alloy is removed from its surface leaving a brilliant .0006 inch 23 K gilt coating. Indeed, this process was used in ancient America. Plus, this surface covering is much easier to engrave. Likewise, pure gold would be too soft to make useful plates. But tumbaga is remarkably tough and resilient.[40]

Not only did Joseph Smith correctly claim that the Book of Mormon was engraved upon metal plates, but the Nephites also could have chosen no better material to vindicate their sacred scripture than tumbaga, which has the "appearance of gold."

63. New World Temples and Towers

According to the Book of Mormon, the Nephites designed their temple after the temple of Solomon. Anthropologist Dr. Sorenson notes the layout of Solomon's temple and how it compares to Mesoamerican temples.

> The temple of Solomon was built on a platform, so people literally went "up" to it. Inside were distinct rooms of differing sacredness. Outside the building itself was a courtyard or plaza surrounded by a wall. Sacrifices were made in that space, atop altars of stepped or terraced form. The levels of the altar structure represented the layered universe as Israelites and other Near Eastern peoples conceived of it. The temple building was oriented so that the rising of the sun on solstice day (either March 21 or September 21) sent the earliest rays—considered "the glory of the Lord"—to shine through the temple doors, which were opened for the occasion, directly into the holiest part. The same features generally characterized Mesoamerican temple [pyramid] complexes. . . . Torquemada, an early Spanish priest in the New World, compared the plan of Mexican temples with that of the temple of Solomon, and a [non-LDS] modern scholar agrees.[41]

Both the early Near Eastern temples and the early American pyramid/temples were of similar construction, design, and purpose. The association of water with temples also has its parallel in both the Old and New Worlds. Water that came from inside the earth was particularly sacred. In both the Old Testament, and the ancient Near East, it was believed that below the earth's surface was a freshwater sea that could potentially burst forth at temples. The temple at Jerusalem was believed to confine these waters from flooding. In a vision, Ezekiel saw a time when life-giving waters would flow as a river from beneath the temple (Ezekiel 47:1–12). These same concepts were believed by the ancient Americans concerning their pyramids. When the natives faced defeat by Cortez and his men, the native priests opened a hole in the wall of the Cholula pyramid, expecting water to flood the structure as their beliefs had implied.[42]

It should be noted that the terms *temples, pyramids, artificial mountains,* and *towers* can all be applied to the same structures in both the Book of Mormon and ancient Mesoamerica. The word *tower* in the Book of Mormon relates to a concept which goes back to Mesopotamia prior to 3000 BC. The "Tower of Babel" of Genesis, and the same "great tower" of Ether, refers the ancient Near Eastern ziggurats (giant platforms with stepped and sloping sides), which measured from 80 to 270 feet high. As Sorenson observes: "It may seem strange to modern readers, used to considering narrow, soaring castle and cathedral spires as 'towers,' that bulky mounds and ziggurats would be termed "towers" by the Book of Mormon scribes. But when the Spanish invaders saw the Mesoamerican temple platforms, they immediately called them torres, 'towers,' so height, not shape, must be the main criterion."[43]

These ziggurats were considered to be artificial mountains upon which deity could dwell or visit men. This same concept was held by the ancient Americans.

64. Mesoamerican Warfare

The Book of Mormon records the history of a people who were often at war with their neighbors—especially when they, themselves, refused to follow the counsel of the Lord. As one anti-Mormon has written: "Thus far no . . . swords, breast-plates, arm shields, [or] armor . . . *have ever been found in pre-colonial archaeological sites.*"[44] The critics contend that not only were many Book of Mormon weapons unknown in early Mesoamerica, but that war itself was virtually unknown: "Archaeologists assert that, during the *Book of Mormon* period, warfare was almost unknown in the Americas, except for ceremonial purposes (as practiced by the Aztecs)."[45]

Although this critic was a little behind the times, until recently, most experts embraced the same view. Even most scholars believed that war among ancient Mesoamerican cultures was "a late exception." The early groups, it was believed, "practiced only the arts of peace." According to more recent studies, this is a complete distortion. "It appears the Mesoamericans probably were never very peaceful."[46] As Howard La Fay of National Geographic explains,

> The light of scholarship has begun to pierce the ancient shadows. . . .
> Gone forever is the image of the Maya as peaceful, rather primitive
> farmers practicing esoteric religious rites in the quiet of their jungles

fastness. What emerges is a portrait of a vivid, warlike race, numerous beyond any previous estimate, employing sophisticated agricultural techniques. And, like the Vikings half a world away, they traded and raided with zest. . . . the Maya—so long portrayed as a peaceful, devout people—were involved in warfare from very early times.[47]

The Book of Mormon claims that the Nephites and Lamanites made use of bows and arrows, swords, and cimeters. The anti-Mormons have claimed that these weapons were unknown in pre-Columbian America. Thanks to the recent findings, however, many non-Mormon archaeologists have concluded just the opposite. The bow, for instance, "was in fact known in Mesoamerica by at least the first millennium BC, precisely as described in the Book of Mormon."[48] Non-Mormon scholar P. Tolstoy claims that the bow was used in ancient America well before 600 BC[49] while recent excavations at Tehuacan valley, Central America, "confirm that the bow was used at least as early as the time of Christ."[50]

As for swords, the most likely candidate would be a weapon known to the Aztecs as the *macuahuitl*—a long wooden shaft with large pieces of obsidian flakes fixed into its edges. Volcanic obsidian is so sharp that it was perfect for using in the construction of swords. Although used by the later Aztecs and Mayans, the macuahuitl dates back to Book of Mormon times. The Book of Mormon tells us that swords were so sharp they could sever limbs with one stroke. At the time of the Spanish conquest, it was recorded that one Mayan warrior cut the head of a Spaniard's horse with one stroke of his macuahuitl or what the Spanish called his "sword."[51]

A cimeter (today know as scimitar) usually refers to a blade which is curved. The Book of Mormon tells us that warriors often fought with both swords and cimeters. It is therefore interesting to note that one recently discovered Mesoamerican sculpture depicts a warrior with a macuahuitl (sword) in one hand and a curved weapon (cimeter) in his other hand. Enough Mesoamerican artwork and artifacts display the basic characteristics of a cimeter, that the Book of Mormon is vindicated for its usage.[52]

The critics have also long laughed at the Book of Mormon's claim that, during battles, the Nephites wore armor and "thick clothing" (see Alma 43:19). The Aztecs and others, however, wore a protective, thick, quilted armor garment called an *ichcauipili,* which could withstand a direct arrow impact. The garment was so light and cheap that the Spaniards adopted it as well.[53]

When modern readers think of "armor," the first thing that usually pops to mind are the metal suits of armor as used in late medieval Western Europe. History has demonstrated, however, that ancient cultures made armor from metal, wood, bone, horn, stone, animal hides, leaves, and even silk.[54] Dr. Hamblin has shown that the Mayan art of Book of Mormon times depicts armor breastplates, head plates, shields, arm shields, and thick protective clothing—all of which are also mentioned in the Book of Mormon. Ancient Mesoamerican armor was usually constructed of wood or bone, yet they qualify as armor nevertheless.[55]

Warfare, swordlike weapons, and armor were all known during Book of Mormon times in Book of Mormon lands. In the case of warfare, the Book of Mormon (and the Prophet Joseph Smith) was once again years ahead of the most learned men of the early 1800s.

65. Seasonality of Warfare

Several years ago, anthropologist Dr. John Sorenson examined the timing of warfare as recorded in the Book of Mormon and discovered that wars took place at specific times during the year rather than randomly.[56] While the Nephites (like most ancient cultures) may not have always used one specific calendar, it seems that for at least some period the Nephites had a twelve month calendar. It's also probable that, like many other ancient societies, the Nephite New Year began in late December during the winter solstice. This was probably changed shortly after Christ's birth when the New Year would have began in April.

When Dr. Sorenson charted the timing of warfare from all known Book of Mormon passages that provided such information, it was discovered that the majority of wars took place between the twelfth and third months (our December through March).

Is the seasonality pattern of warfare accidental, or was there a reason why most of the wars took place during the same months of the year? In ancient societies food was typically the most important factor in determining the schedule for wars. The soldiers of ancient armies where generally average citizens who farmed during the year to support themselves and their families. To leave for war during the cultivating or harvesting season would have meant no food during their battles, and no food for their fellow citizens back home.

The Book of Mormon (especially the book of Alma) tells us that the middle of the calendar year was the growing season, while the harvesting season came near the end of the year. From other textual clues it seems that months four through nine (our April through September) were the season for cultivating crops. The harvest would likely have occurred from October through early December, which would have left late December through March open for scheduling wars. The Book of Mormon's consistency in the timing war is, of itself, a remarkable feat.

The other major factor in determining the timing of wars is weather conditions. The rainy season takes place during the growing season—and provides another reason why ancient soldiers would have avoided battle during this time of year. Armies would rather fight during dry (yet hopefully cool) seasons because it's easier to travel on dirt than in mud and easier to fight and camp when supplies are not wet. In Enos 1:20 and Alma 3:5 (as well as in other verses) we find that the Lamanites traveled virtually naked to campaign against the Nephites. This would have been unlikely had they traveled in cold or rainy months.

Many LDS scholars believe that the Book of Mormon events took place in a limited area in Mesoamerica. When we examine the history of ancient Mesoamericans, we find some nice correlations to what is written in the Book of Mormon. In Yucatan, for instance, wars were usually fought between October and January, and may have lasted as late as February in other Mesoamerican regions. Maize—the staple of Mesoamerican diet—was planted in April or May just before the rainy season. The wettest months are July through September, and crops are typically harvested from October to December.

It's nearly impossible that Joseph Smith knew that much about the seasonality of Mesoamerican warfare or the monthly war and crop cycles in Mesoamerica, since very little was known about Mesoamerica in his day. While there is evidence that Joseph speculated as to the location and geography of Book of Mormon events, he may have assumed—like many of the contemporary Saints—that Book of Mormon events took place in the New England area, or at least in the United States. If Joseph was the author rather than the translator of the Book of Mormon, it seems reasonable to conclude that he would have incorporated his understanding of climate and warfare into his novel.

In Alma 51, however, we read of a major battle that took place at the end of the year (or around December). In verses 32 through 33 we read that the armies were camped on "the borders on the beach" by the east coast and both armies were exhausted because of their "labors and heat of the day." "Heat of the day" in December on the East Coast of the United States? Had Joseph Smith been the author of the book he would either have had them fighting in the summer or would have had them bundled for the freezing East Coast December winters. Instead, what we find in the Book of Mormon is an internally consistent pattern that accurately matches what we would expect to find among real ancient Mesoamericans who planned their battles.

66. Cement

In about AD 49, after many decades of peace, contentions began to rise among the people in Zarahemla. The problem was so bad that many dissenters left Zarahemla and moved northward. In their new location they began to build homes out of cement (Helaman 3:7). According to the critics, and what was known about ancient America during Joseph Smith's day, the Native Americans did not work in cement. According to recent research, however, some Mesoamericans began using cement extensively at about the time indicated in the Book of Mormon: "One of the most notable uses of cement is in the temple complex at Teotihuacan, north of present-day Mexico City. According to David S. Hyman, the structural use of cement appears suddenly in the archaeological record. Its earliest sample 'is a fully developed product.' The cement floor slabs at this site 'were remarkably high in structural quality.' Although exposed to the elements for nearly two thousand years, they still 'exceed many present-day building code requirements.' "[57]

Because Mesoamerican cement is almost exclusively lime cement,[58] and because Mesoamerica is typically heavily forested, tons of trees had to be cut in order to produce, maintain, and repair lime cement. This eventually caused a problem of deforestation. Deforestation can eventually cause local climate changes, and it was the cause for the collapse of many ancient American cities. Such was the fate of Tikal—a once-powerful New World city that collapsed in the tenth century.

Deforestation was probably a major factor in the downfall of Teotihuacan (which was contemporary with Book of Mormon times and in the right location for dissidents to have emigrated after leaving the likely location of Zarahemla). Teotihuacan was also constructed of cement from at least AD 250 (and the Nephites continued to live in their new territory for many centuries).

Mormon, as an editor writing about three centuries after the emigration from Zarahemla, and writing according to his world view of history, says that the people used cement because the land was devoid of trees. In Mormon's world, the new city was not only devoid of trees but constructed of cement. This accurately describes—including the time period and location—the ancient city of Teotihuacan. Mormon, however, was likely mistaken on which element caused the other. The Nephites wouldn't have had a lack of trees until they deforested the land to make the cement. The desolation of trees would have followed the deforestation to make cement.[59]

67. Barley

Among the list of supposed Book of Mormon blunders is barley:

> There should be at last one example of Old World-type plants (especially grains) [as] noted in the Book of Mormon.[60]

> *Barley never grew in the New World* before the white man brought it here.[61]

> Botanical problems . . . [are] encountered when . . . Barley is mentioned in Mosiah 9:9.[62]

In truth barley was unknown in the New World when discovered by the Europeans. It is entirely possible, however, that this grain had disappeared not long after Book of Mormon times. When the Spanish came to the New World in the sixteenth century, Bishop Landa wrote how they helped the Indians to raise European millet which grew marvelously well in the area. Four centuries later, however, botanists were unable to find even a trace of the millet about which Landa had written.[63] Imported crops don't always yield good seeds.

It's also easy to understand how such a useful grain could have fallen prey to the same linguistic problems as the animal kingdom. In America *corn* refers to maize; but in England it means wheat; and in Scotland oats. Likewise, *barley* could have been used as a label for another grain in ancient America.

In an article in *Science 83*, Daniel B. Adams wrote of the archaeological research of the Hohokam Indians—a pre-Columbian culture that lived in Arizona from about 300 BC to AD 1450 and had been influenced by Mesoamerica. According to Adams: "The most startling evidence of Hohokam agricultural sophistication came . . . when . . . archaeologists found preserved grain of what looks like domesticated barley, the first ever found in the New World. Wild barleys have a fibrous husk over each grain. Domesticated barley lack this. So does the Hohokam barley. . . . Nearly half the samples from one site yielded barley."[64]

As Dr. Sorenson was quick to point out: "That such an important [discovery] could have gone undiscovered for so long by archaeologists justifies the thought that wheat might also be found in ancient sites."[65]

Adams also explains that the barley may have come from Mexico, and in Alma 63:6–10 we read of various Nephite migrations to the North that might have influenced North American cultures and crops.

Actually, to the surprise of many Mormons (and even more of a surprise to the anti-Mormons), the find at the Hohokam site in Arizona was a first only because it yielded "cultivated" or "domesticated" barley. Biologist Howard Stutz recently disclosed that "three types of *wild* barley have long been known to be native to the Americas."[66] Furthermore, scholars now report that other examples of what may be "domesticated" barley have been found in Eastern Oklahoma and Southern Illinois, dating from AD 1 to AD 900.[67] The Book of Mormon has been correct all along in claiming that barley was known anciently in the New World.

68. List of Book of Mormon Items

Critics frequently claim that the Book of Mormon is contradicted by New World archaeology. This may have been true in 1830 when the Book of Mormon was published, but it is no longer true today. Professional archaeologist Dr. John Clark of the New World Archaeological Foundation recently compiled a list of sixty items mentioned in the Book of Mormon. The list includes items such as steel, swords, barley, cement, thrones, literacy, and more. A dozen years after the Book of Mormon was printed, only eight (or 13.3 percent) of those sixty items had been confirmed by archaeological evidence—in other words, archaeology did not support the Book of Mormon by the mid-nineteenth century.

By the turn of the twenty-first century, however, forty-five of those sixty items (or 75 percent) have been confirmed by archaeological evidence. Thirty-five of the list's items (58 percent) have seen definite confirmation, while ten items (17 percent) have received tentative confirmation. Obviously, archaeology is an ongoing discipline, and new discoveries continue to come forth. It is entirely possible that nearly all of the items on the list may some day be confirmed by archaeological evidence. If no more items are discovered, however, that doesn't mean that those things didn't exist; it simply means that they still lay hidden. In contrast to what was known about the ancient New World in Joseph Smith's day, modern archaeology supports the items listed in the Book of Mormon.[68]

Dr. Cyrus Gordon, former chairman of the Department of Mediterranean Studies at Brandeis University, said: "I am speaking academically and am not qualified to speak on the Book of Mormon itself. If I were to do that I would study it for three years before commenting. But there are many points in archaeology in its favor."[69]

69. Tree of Life, Part 2

Earlier it was shown that the "tree of life" vision as recorded in the Book of Mormon has definite similarities to certain Old World traditions and is very much at home in the ancient Near East. Recent findings also show that the tree of life motif and Lehi's vision of that tree are every bit at home in the ancient New World as well. "Of the three known Maya codices [books]," notes Irene Woodford, "two, namely the *Codex Dresdensis* and the *Codex Tro-Cortesianus,* portray the so-called

Tree of Life. . . . The *Dresden Codex* was discovered in Vienna, Austria, in 1839, and was given to the Royal Library, now known as the State Library, at Dresden, Germany, where it remains today. . . . The *Codex Tro-Cortesianus* was discovered in Spain in the 1860's in two separate sections."[70]

Neither codex was known at the time the Book of Mormon was published.

70. Uto-Aztecan Language

When the Lehites arrived in the new world over two thousand years ago, they would have merged with existing native populations. Typically, when a small group melds with a larger group, the smaller group adopts the custom and language of the larger group. Within a few generations, the spoken language of the Nephites and Lamanites would likely have become that of their neighbors. It's also possible, however, that some of the original Hebrew words used by the Lehites were picked up by their neighbors and continued to be used even after the Hebrew language disappeared.

Near Eastern language expert Dr. Brian Stubbs argues for a possible link between Uto-Aztecan (a family of about thirty Native American languages) and Hebrew. As a professional linguist, Stubbs avoids the pitfalls of amateurs who simply point to similar words between two different languages. All languages can have a few similar words by pure chance. Linguists have the training and methodology to look for those words that are genetically related.

Using the methodology and professional tools of his trade, Dr. Stubbs has uncovered thousands of Uto-Aztecan (UA)/Hebrew word pairs. Even some non-LDS linguists have taken notice. Dr. Roger West-cott—Professor Emeritus of Anthropology and Linguistics at Drew University—expressed his favorable opinion of Stubbs's research. Stubbs's examples are not merely coincidental, he noted, but instead follow "systematic sound-shifts" and other linguistic models just as we find present in the studies of other known language family connections.[71]

71. Earthquakes and Volcanoes

In approximately 6 BC, Samuel, the Lamanite prophet, prophesied of Christ's birth and death and revealed that when the Savior died there would be three days of darkness, great upheavals, and destruction. About forty years later, at the time of Christ's crucifixion, the Nephites saw the fulfillment of this prophecy (see Helaman 14). Chapter 8 of 3 Nephi records the great calamities that befell the Nephites and Lamanites at the time of Christ's death. First there arose a great storm—a tempest—with thunder, "insomuch that it did shake the whole earth as if it was about to divide asunder" (v. 6). There were lightnings, whirlwinds, and fires, and cities sank into the sea. The earthquake caused major destruction and death.

"And it came to pass that there was thick darkness upon all the face of the land, insomuch that the inhabitants thereof who had not fallen could feel the vapor of darkness; and there could be no light, because of the darkness, neither candles, neither torches; neither could there be fire kindled with their fine and exceedingly dry wood, so that there could not be any light at all" (vv. 20–21).

Darkness prevailed for three days. From a scientific point of view, the calamities which would fit the description of destruction recorded in 3 Nephi would have to be an earthquake followed by a volcanic eruption—which we now know can be triggered by earthquakes.

Since the Book of Mormon likely took place in ancient Mesoamerica, it's of interest to note that Mesoamerica lies in an active earthquake zone—a fact that would have been unknown to Joseph Smith. First, the Book of Mormon tells us that a great storm arose which apparently turned into a hurricane (see vv. 5–6). According to research, many great earthquakes, such as the earthquake in Japan of 1923, are preceded by great storms. Some specialists believe that certain weather conditions may trigger earthquakes. Second, the Book of Mormon tells us that a "terrible thunder" preceded the quaking (v. 6). Once again, modern studies show that deafening roars often herald a great quake. Next, the Book of Mormon tells us that cities caught fire (v. 8). As reports have demonstrated today, fires not only follow major earthquakes, but more often then not, cause as much or more destruction than the quakes themselves.[72]

Volcanic activity also contributed to the destruction of Nephite cities and typically earthquakes and activity of nearby volcanoes coincide with one another. Archaeological evidence also indicates that those areas encompassed by Book of Mormon lands were subjected to a volcanic eruption and widespread destruction at around the time of Christ's crucifixion.[73]

For example, at the site of Chalchuapa—near the border of Guatemala, and situated in proposed Book of Mormon territory—we find a layer of volcanic ash in a strata dated to AD 30. In another area in El Salvador, an archaeological site was buried under thick layers of ash around the time of Christ. In Copilco, archaeologist found lava flow thirty feet thick that date to about AD 30.[74] Anthropologist Dr. Sorenson describes the effects of a modern volcanic eruption in Mesoamerica.

> A description of the eruption of Consequina volcano in Nicaragua in 1835 hints at the terror and destruction that resulted from the powerful disaster at the time of Christ. A dense cloud first rose above the cone, and within a couple of hours it "enveloped everything in the greatest darkness, so that the nearest objects were imperceptible." Fear-struck wild animals blundered into settlements, adding to the terror. Then came quakes, "a perpetual undulation." Volcanic ash began to fall, like "fine powder-like flour." The thunder and lightning "continued the whole night and the following day." Dust thrown up into the atmosphere combined with heat from the volcano to trigger the storms. Still later the worst tremor of all hit, strong enough to throw people to the ground. Darkness again came on and this time lasted forty-three hours. These conditions, multiplied in both intensity and territory covered, sound much like 3 Nephi.[75]

The Book of Mormon records that a "thick darkness" a "vapor of darkness" (vv. 20–22) caused deaths (3 Nephi 10:13). Following the volcanic activity in Pompeii, many victims died of suffocation when they were covered with volcanic ash (vapor of darkness).[76] According to the Book of Mormon, not only did this darkness extinguish life, but it also extinguished fires (8:20–22). One critic asked: "In describing Christ's crucifixion 3 Nephi 8:20–23 says that the darkness was so great for three days [sic] that the candles and torches could not give off light! Why not?"[77]

The vapor of ash and smoke was so thick that there was not enough air to breathe, let alone kindle fires. According to scholars, a volcanic disaster on the Greek island of Thera in 1400 BC caused an "overpowering thickness of the air" which "must have extinguished all lamps."[78] Likewise, Russell Ball suggests that the volcano may have caused a dense concentration of volcanic gases (carbon dioxide and sulfur dioxide), which would have been sufficient in preventing the igniting of kindling. Heavy fall of volcanic ash would have prevented ignition from the sparks of flint (most likely the means of starting fires) and could explain the Book of Mormon's terms "mists of darkness" and "vapor of darkness." Such heavy ash and volcanic gases would also have caused suffocation. Ball also notes that the "uncle of Pliny died of suffocation as a consequence of a volcanic eruption."[79]

The Book of Mormon also tells us that during the destruction several cities were buried in the sea (3 Nephi 8:9, 9:4–6, 8). We know now that earthquakes can also trigger tsunamis—giant waves of water that can wipe out entire cities. In 2004, for example, an earthquake in the Indian Ocean caused a tsunami that had waves one hundred feet high, which crashed over coastal cities, killing nearly a quarter of a million people in eleven countries.[80]

72. Four Hundred Year Baktun

The Nephites prophesied that within four hundred years after the coming of Christ, the people would turn to wickedness and be destroyed (see Alma 45:10, Helaman 13:9, and Mormon 8:6). What makes this interesting is that the time-obsessed Maya measured time by a four hundred-year interval known as a *baktun*. The baktun was made up of the extremely important twenty-year sub-interval known as a *katun*.[81] Not only do we find the four hundred year baktun in the verses mentioned above, but Moroni bids us farewell "four hundred and twenty years"—or one katun after the final baktun—following "the sign" that "was given of the coming of Christ" (Moroni 10:1).[82]

73. Mesoamerican Demographic and History Cycles

The Book of Mormon tells the story of two primary civilizations—the Jaredites and descendants of the Lehites. The Jaredites came to the Americas in about 2200 BC and were mostly destroyed in about 400 BC. The Nephites flourished in the New World from about 600 BC until about AD 400. Because LDS scholars believe that the Jaredites and Nephites were not alone in the New World, it seems reasonable to assume that other cultures would have flourished before, during, and after Book of Mormon times. When we examine the ancient Mesoamerican civilization cycles—by way of rise and decline of cities—we find some interesting parallels.

The Mesoamerican Olmec cities, for instance, came to life in about 1700 BC and were abandoned—under duress—in about 400 BC. A rough assessment of the growth and decline of Olmec populations correctly matches what we find in Jaredite history. This civilization was replaced by the lowland Maya who began building cities in about 400 BC and then experienced a mini-collapse in about AD 200. "In short," noted professional Mesoamerican archaeologist, Dr. John Clark, "the correspondences between the Book of Mormon and cycles of Mesoamerican civilization are striking."[83]

NOTES

1. Quoted in Matthew Roper, "Limited Geography and the Book of Mormon: Historical Antecedents and Early Interpretations," *The FARMS Review* 16, no. 2 (2004): 259.

2. John E. Clark, "Archaeological Trends and Book of Mormon Origins," *The Worlds of Joseph Smith*, 89.

3. John E. Clark, "Archaeology, Relics, and Book of Mormon Belief," *Journal of Book of Mormon Studies* 14, no. 2 (2005): 48.

4. Ibid., 49.

5. Quoted in Michael R. Ash, *Shaken Faith Syndrome: Strengthening One's Testimony in the Face of Criticism and Doubt* (Redding, CA: FAIR, 2008), 100.

6. Hugh W. Nibley, *The Book of Mormon and the Ruins: The Main Issues* (Provo, UT: FARMS, 1983), 1.

7. Vestal and Wallace, *The Firm Foundation of Mormonism*, 103.

8. George E. Stuart, "The Maya Riddle of the Glyphs," *National Geographic,* December 1975, 769.

9. V. Garth Norman, "San Lorenzo as the Jaredite City of Lib," *Newsletter and Proceedings of the Society for Early Historic Archaeology,* June 1983, 4.

10. Sorenson, "How Could Joseph Smith Write So Accurately about Ancient American Civilizations," 262.

11. David A. Palmer, "A Survey of Pre-1830 Historical Sources Relating to the Book of Mormon," *BYU Studies* 17, no. 1 (Autumn 1976): 107.

12. T. Patrick Culbert, "Maya Treasures of an Ancient Civilization," *Archaeology* (March/April 1985), 60.

13. Palmer, "A Survey of Pre-1830 Historical Sources Relating to the Book of Mormon," *BYU Studies,* 106–107.

14. Martin, *The Kingdom of the Cults,* 162.

15. John L. Sorenson, *An Ancient American Setting for the Book of Mormon* (Salt Lake City, UT: Deseret Book; Provo, UT: FARMS, 1985), 235.

16. John L. Sorenson, "The Book of Mormon as Mesoamerican Codex," Newsletter and Proceedings of the S.E.H.A. (December 1976), 4–5.

17. Sorenson, "How Could Joseph Smith Write So Accurately about Ancient American Civilizations," 266–67.

18. Ibid., 298.

19. Ibid., 298–99.

20. Wallace E. Hunt, Jr., "The Marketplace," *Journal of Book of Mormon Studies* 4, no. 2 (1995): 138.

21. Ibid., 140.

22. Key, *A Biologist Examines the Book of Mormon,* 2.

23. Sorenson, *An Ancient American Setting for the Book of Mormon,* 53.

24. Ibid., 352–53.

25. Ibid., 201.

26. Morell, "The Lost Language of Coba," 52.

27. Howard W. Goodkind, "Lord Kingsborough Lost His Fortune Trying to Prove the Maya Were Descendants of the Ten Lost Tribes," *Biblical Archaeology Review* (September/October 1985), 62.

28. Cheesman, *Ancient Writing on Metal Plates,* 25.

29. Gardner, *Second Witness: Analytical and Contextual Commentary on the Book of Mormon,* 1:25; Morell, "The Lost Language of Coba," 48.

30. Joseph Smith, *Times and Seasons* 3, no 9 (1 March 1842), 707.

31. Hyde, *Mormonism: Its Leaders and Designs,* 244.

32. Whalen, *The Latter-day Saints in the Modern Day World,* 27.

33. Robert F. Smith, "The 'Golden' Plates," *Reexploring the Book of Mormon,* 276.

34. Read H. Putnam, "Were the Golden Plates Made of Tumbaga?" *Improvement Era,* Sept. 1966, 829–30.

35. Heather Lechtman, "Pre-Columbian Surface Metallurgy," *Scientific America,* June 1984, 56.

36. Ibid., 60.

37. Reprinted in *Early Mormon Documents,* 1:505.

38. Putnam, "Were the Golden Plates Made of Tumbaga?" 789, 828–29.

39. Ibid., 830–31.

40. "The 'Golden' Plates," *FARMS Updates,* October 1984.

41. Sorenson, *An Ancient American Setting for the Book of Mormon,* 143.

42. Ibid., 176, 179.

43. Ibid., 174.

44. Martin, *The Kingdom of the Cults,* 163; emphasis added.

45. Scott, *The Mormon Mirage,* 83.

46. Sorenson, *An Ancient American Setting for the Book of Mormon,* 260.

47. Howard La Fay, "The Maya, Children of Time," *National Geographic,* December 1975, 732–33.

48. William J. Hamblin, "The Bow and Arrow in the Book of Mormon," *Warfare in the Book of Mormon,* eds., Stephen D. Ricks and William J. Hamblin (Salt Lake City, UT: Deseret Book; Provo, UT: FARMS, 1990), 385.

49. Ibid., 379.

50. Sorenson, *An Ancient American Setting for the Book of Mormon,* 262; William Hamblin, *Handheld Weapons in the Book of Mormon,* (Provo, UT: FARMS, 1985), 14.

51. Sorenson, *An Ancient American Setting for the Book of Mormon,* 262.

52. Hamblin, *Handheld Weapons in the Book of Mormon,* 33.

53. Sorenson, *An Ancient American Setting for the Book of Mormon,* 262.

54. William J. Hamblin, "Armor in the Book of Mormon," *Warfare in the Book of Mormon,* 402.

55. Ibid., 405–18.

56. John L. Sorenson, "Seasonality of Warfare in the Book of Mormon and in Mesoamerica," *Warfare in the Book of Mormon,* 445–78.

57. Matthew G. Wells and John W. Welch, "Concrete Evidence for the

Book of Mormon," *Reexploring the Book of Mormon,* 212–13.

58. Ibid., 213.

59. Gardner, *Second Witness: Analytical and Contextual Commentary on the Book of Mormon,* 5:61–64.

60. Scott, *The Mormon Mirage,* 81.

61. Ibid., 82; italics in original.

62. Key, *A Biologist Examines the Book of Mormon,* 1.

63. Sorenson, *An Ancient American Setting for the Book of Mormon,* 139.

64. Daniel B. Adams, "Last Ditch Archaeology," *Science 83,* December 1983, 32.

65. Sorenson, *An Ancient American Setting for the Book of Mormon,* 184.

66. "Barley in Ancient America," *FARMS Updates,* Dec. 1984.

67. Ibid.

68. John E. Clark, "Debating the Foundations of Mormonism: Archaeology and the Book of Mormon," at http://fairlds.org/FAIR_ Conferences/2005_Debating_the_Foundations_of_Mormonism.html (accessed 20 March 2008).

69. Wirth, *A Challenge to the Critics,* 20.

70. Irene Briggs Woodford, "The 'Tree of Life' in Ancient America: Its Representations and Significance," *Bulletin of the University Archaeological Society* (1953), 3.

71. Brian Darrel Stubbs, "Looking Over vs. Overlooking Native American Languages: Let's Void the Void," *Journal of Book of Mormon Studies* 5, no. 1 (1996): 1–49.

72. Nibley, *Since Cumorah,* 263–64.

73. Sorenson, *An Ancient American Setting,* 321; Bruce W. Warren and Thomas Stuart Ferguson, *The Messiah in Ancient America* (Provo, UT: Book of Mormon Research Foundation, 1987), 39.

74. Warren and Ferguson, *The Messiah in Ancient America,* 43–44.

75. Sorenson, *An Ancient American Setting,* 321.

76. Nibley, *Since Cumorah,* 266.

77. Key, *A Biologist Examines the Book of Mormon,* 2.

78. Nibley, *Since Cumorah,* 267.

79. Russell H. Ball, "An Hypothesis Concerning the Three Days of Darkness Among the Nephites," *Journal of Book of Mormon Studies* 2, no. 1 (Spring 1993): 110.

80. See http://en.wikipedia.org/wiki/2004_Indian_Ocean_earthquake

MICHAEL R. ASH

(accessed 6 July 2008); for more examples see John A. Tvedtnes, "Historical Parallels to the Destruction at the Time of the Crucifixion," *Journal of Book of Mormon Studies* 3, no. 1 (1994): 177–79.

81. See George E. Stuart, "The Maya Riddle of the Glyphs," *National Geographic,* December 1975, 785.

82. John E. Clark, "Archaeology, Relics, and Book of Mormon Belief," 46–47.

83. Ibid., 48.

Book of Abraham

74. Ur and Olishem

The Bible tells us that God "didst choose Abram, and broughtest him forth out of Ur of the Chaldees, and gavest him the name of Abraham" (Nehemiah 9:7). Where exactly is Ur of the Chaldees? For the past century, most experts have suggested that it was in southern Iraq in what is now known as Tell al-Muqayyar. Joseph Smith's translation of the Book of Abraham, however, tells us that Ur was heavily influenced by Egypt during Abraham's day (about 2000 BC) and scholars don't think this was the case in Tell al-Muqayyar.

More recent scholarship suggests that Ur might have been in northern Syria and southern Turkey in a place known anciently as Aram-Naharaim (northwestern Mesopotamia in ancient times). Not coincidentally, ancient Aram-Naharaim was under the influence of Egypt during the days of Abraham. An added layer of support comes from the Book of Abraham's mention of "the plain of Olishem" (Abraham 1:10), which apparently was part of the land of Chaldea. While the Bible never mentions such a place, scholars have recently discovered an inscription of the name Olishem dating to about 2250 BC in northwestern Syria—just where we would expect to find it according to Joseph Smith.[1]

75. Heliocentric Universe

Surprisingly, one of the more interesting evidences for the antiquity of the Book of Abraham comes from the field of astronomy. In Joseph Smith's day most Americans believed that the sun revolved around the earth, but that the sun was also the center of the universe (this is known as heliocentricity). Today, of course, we realize that the sun is not the center of the universe but is the center of our solar system.

According to ancient cosmologies, it was believed that the earth was the center of the universe; nothing existed below the earth, and the heavens—or "expanse"—was situated above the earth and was composed of multiple tiered layers. The moon was in one layer, the sun in a higher layer, and the stars in the highest layer of all. We find this same concept in the book of Abraham (see 3:5, 9, and 17). Since everything orbits the earth, the higher the object in the sky, the longer it took to circle the earth and therefore higher objects had greater lengths of "reckoning" (compare to Abraham 3:5).

In Abraham 3:8–9, we read that "there shall be another planet whose reckoning of time shall be longer still; And thus there shall be the reckoning of the time of one planet above another, until thou come nigh unto Kolob." Since stars were the furthest from the earth, it made sense that they were also nearest to God. In the Book of Abraham, the star Kolob is the star nearest "the throne of God" (Abraham 3:9).

We find the same teachings in some ancient texts. In the Apocalypse of Abraham, for example (which dates from about the same time period as the Book of Abraham papyri but was not discovered until much later), we read that God's throne is said to reside in the eighth firmament ("firmaments" being another term for the varying tiers in the heavens above the Earth).[2]

According to the Book of Abraham, the highest celestial objects "govern" the objects below them (see Abraham 3:3, 9 and Facsimile 2, fig. 5). Likewise, when we turn to the Apocalypse of Abraham, we find that God's throne is in the highest of heavens and that His commands are passed down by angels through the various levels of heaven. Each of the higher levels governs and commands the lower levels.

While such a cosmology makes little sense from the heliocentric cosmology of Joseph Smith's milieu, it makes perfect sense from the ancient cosmologies accepted by the ancient people of the Near East. But if Abraham's cosmology was false, why would God teach Abraham a false cosmology? As one scholar who has studied the issue explains: "The purpose of the revelation of astronomical ideas is not necessarily to give Abraham an accurate view of the universe but to provide him a mechanism to attract the attention of Pharaoh [see Abraham 3:15]. In such circumstances it would make sense for Abraham to be given a geocentric astronomy that would have been intelligible to people of his day."[3]

God speaks to mankind in our language using symbols and ideas that we can comprehend. Although Abraham used the Urim and Thummim to "talk" with God, there is no indication that his view of the universe was visionary. Instead, the actual text suggests that Abraham was standing on the Earth, looking into the night sky. From Abraham's view, the heavens did revolve around the Earth. For God's purpose—and since there is no single privileged point for observing the cosmos—Abraham's perspective was as good as was needed.

The remarkable thing is that Joseph Smith correctly translated the ancient cosmological view as it would have been understood by Abraham, rather than incorporating his own nineteenth-century cosmology as an author would have done.

76. More Book of Abraham Evidences

Following are several additional evidences for things in the Book of Abraham that Joseph apparently got right. It's important to point out once again that no one in America in Joseph Smith's day knew enough Egyptian to correctly translate what was on the papyri.

In Book of Abraham, Facsimile 1, figure 11 is said to "represent the pillars of heaven as understood by the Egyptians." When we turn to non-Biblical ancient texts, we find support for this interpretation. The phrase "pillars of heaven" even occurs several times in Egyptian literature.

Figure 1 in Facsimile 2 is said to represent Kolob and signifies "the first creation, nearest to the celestial, or the residence of God." Ancient Egyptians understood that this character was symbolic of God, seated at the center of the universe and endowed with the primeval creative force. The word *Kolob* most likely derives from the common Semitic root *QLB*, which means "heart, center, middle." Qalb, which is the Arabic form of the word, is used for some of the brightest stars in the night's sky. Also in figure 1, Joseph Smith says the Egyptians called the Earth *Jah-oh-eh*. The actual Egyptian word for the Earth is pronounced "yoh-heh."

Figure 4, according to Joseph Smith, is said to represent the expanse of the heavens, the revolutions of Kolob and Obilish, and also the number one thousand. Egyptologists tell us that this figure is the "hawk-god, Horus-Sokar. Horus was a personification of the sky, and Sokar was associated with the revolution of the Sun and other celestial bodies. Finally, the ship here shown is described in Egyptian texts as 'ship of a thousand.' "[4]

Figure 6 depicts four animal-like mummies (in the upside down portion of the facsimile) which we are told represents "the earth in its four quarters." Egyptologists tell us that the figures represent the four sons of Horus who were not only gods of the four quarters of the earth, but also presided over the four cardinal points.[5]

For more than a century, critics have been claiming that no Egyptian text would have anything to do with Abraham—especially in relation to a lion-couch scene (as we find in Facsimile 1). This can no longer be claimed, however, since the discovery of a lion-couch scene that specifically mentions the Abraham of the Bible.[6] We also now have several ancient Egyptian records that mention the prophet Abraham.[7]

Many unique elements in the Book of Abraham's account of Abraham are missing from the Bible. In 2001 a group of Near Eastern scholars published their research of the dozens of ancient sources that parallel those unique elements. While these elements are missing from the Bible, they *are found* in a variety of ancient Jewish, Muslim, and Christian traditions.

Such common elements are as follows: Abraham's fathers were idol worshippers; idols were made of wood and stone; Terah, Abraham's father, worshiped idols; Terah repented, gave up idol worshipping, but eventually returned to his idols; children were sacrificed by the idol-worshipping Egyptians; those who did not worship idols were killed; Abraham refused to worship idols so he was taken away to be killed or sacrificed; Abraham's own father was behind the attempt to kill Abraham; Abraham was fastened or bound by his captors; Abraham prayed when his life was in danger; an angel came to rescue Abraham; God rescued Abraham from death; the altar (in most cases a furnace in the ancient texts) and the idols were destroyed; the priest (or leader) was smitten and died; Abraham was heir to the priesthood of his ancestors; Abraham held the priesthood; Abraham was linked to Noah; believers become the seed of Abraham and are blessed through him; Abraham sought God earnestly; Abraham made converts in Haran (the city in which they settled after leaving Ur); Abraham possessed the Urim and Thummim, which allowed him to receive revelation from God; Abraham gained knowledge about astronomy from ancient records and God; Abraham taught astronomy to the Egyptians; the Earth has four quarters; Abraham knew about the creation and the fact that there was advance planning; Abraham knew that the elements of the earth obeyed God; Abraham saw the premortal spirits; God instructed Abraham to say that Sarah was his sister; Abraham possessed records from the fathers; Abraham left a record of his own; the Book of Abraham talks about the founding of Egypt; Pharaoh was a descendant of Ham but also of Canaan; the first pharaoh was a good man and was blessed by Noah; Abraham was allowed to sit on the king's throne; there was a famine in Abraham's homeland; Abraham prayed to God for an end of famine; while Genesis says that Abraham was seventy-five when he left Haran, the Book of Abraham and the ancient texts agree that he was actually sixty-two; and Abraham became like God.[8]

Non-LDS Near Eastern scholar David Noel Freedman said that he had never encountered an Abraham account where the patriarch himself was threatened with sacrifice until he saw the claim in the Book of Abraham. Upon further reflection he acknowledged that a similar tradition existed in an ancient Abrahamic document, but an English translation was not available until the 1890s.[9] What are the chances that Joseph could have gotten so many things right by mere guesswork?

NOTES

1. Daniel C. Peterson, "News From Antiquity," *Ensign,* Jan. 1994, 16, 18.
2. John Gee, William J. Hamblin, and Daniel C. Peterson, " 'And I Saw the Stars': The Book of Abraham and Ancient Geocentric Astronomy,"

Astronomy, Papyrus, and Covenant, eds. John Gee and Brian M. Hauglid (Provo, UT: FARMS, 2005), 9.

3. Ibid., 3.

4. Michael D. Rhodes, "The Book of Abraham: Divinely Inspired Scripture," *FARMS Review* (1992) 4:126.

5. Ibid.

6. John Gee, "Abraham in Ancient Egyptian Texts," *Ensign,* July 1992, 60–62.

7. Personal email from John Gee, 20 July 2006.

8. John A. Tvedtnes, Brian M. Hauglid, and John Gee, *Traditions About the Early Life of Abraham* (Provo, UT: FARMS, 2001), 537–53.

9. David Noel Freedman, "The Ebla Tablets and the Abraham Tradition," *Reflections on Mormonism: Judaeo-Christian Parallels,* ed., Truman G. Madsen (Salt Lake City, UT: Bookcraft, 1978), 67.

Doctrines

77. The Apostasy

The Apostasy was already under way while some of the Apostles still lived and they warned that worse times would come after they were gone. As long as they were around, they could correct erroneous doctrines and confound false teachers, but they knew and prophesied of times to come when the Church would go astray. Jude said that believers should "contend for the faith" because, unaware to members, "certain men" were creeping into the fold and trying to pervert the faith (Jude 1:3–4). Peter warns that there are "false prophets also among the people" and "false teachers" would arise from among the members (2 Peter 2:1). Paul prophesied that after his departing, "grievous wolves" would enter the fold and would not spare the flock. He also said that from among the believers, false teachers would arise, perverting the truth and drawing away the disciples (Acts 20:29–30). To the Galatians he wrote: "I marvel that ye are so soon removed from him that called you into the grace of Christ unto another gospel: Which is not another; but there be some that trouble you, and would pervert the gospel of Christ" (Galatians 1:6–7).

In AD 67, Paul wrote a second letter to his beloved friend Timothy wherein he complained that "perilous times" were approaching (2 Timothy 3:1–5). This second letter was penned while Paul was awaiting execution in Rome. Thirteen years earlier, Paul had taught the gospel in Asia and converted many people (Acts 19:8–22). Now, however, he wrote to

Timothy "that all they which are in Asia be turned away from me" (2 Timothy 1:15). Paul spoke of the apostasy as having already begun. He also noted that things would continue to get worse. "For the time will come," Paul wrote to Timothy, "when they [the members of the Church] will not endure sound doctrine; but after their own lusts shall they heap to themselves teachers, having itching ears; and they shall turn away their ears from the truth, and shall be turned unto fables" (2 Timothy 4:3–4). Richard Anderson comments on this scripture: " 'Having itching ears' describes the false teachers in this English translation, but in Greek the participle can only modify 'they.' That is, Christian believers (the topic of Timothy's instructions) will have fickle ears for new teachers that please them. The result is simply corruption of the Christian gospel."[1]

Members in the early Church would seek for teachers who taught only what they wanted to hear. When Paul spoke of Christ's Second Coming, he said, "Let no man deceive you by any means: for that day [the Second Coming] shall not come, except there come a falling away first" (2 Thessalonians 2:3). The term *falling away* comes from the Greek *apostasia*, which has a stronger meaning than just "falling away." The word actually means "apostasy" or "defection from truth."[2]

In approximately AD 96, John, writing the Book of Revelation, chastised all but two of the seven churches in Asia and said that one of the righteous two would suffer martyrdom (Revelation 2–3). Bible scholars have often noted the negativism or sense of an immediate end which is portrayed in many New Testament books, especially in the works of John (1, 2, and 3 John, and Revelation). John speaks of *his* time as the last days: "Little children, it is the last time: and as ye have heard that antichrist shall come, even now are there many antichrists; *whereby we know that it is the last time.* They went out from us, but they were not of us; for if they had been of us, they would no doubt have continued with us: but they went out, that they might be made manifest that they were not all of us" (1 John 2:18–19; italics added).

Anderson indicates that John's letters refer "to the coming of the anti-Christ (not the coming of Christ) by saying that it is 'the last time' (literally, 'the last hour') because there are so many anti-Christs who "went out from us.' (1 John 2:18–19)"[3] This "last time" theme is so dominant in John's writings that some scholars have mistakenly been lead to conclude that John thought Christ's return was imminent. It was the apostasy that was imminent, however, not the Second Coming.

78. Plain and Precious Parts

During Nephi's vision of the tree of life, he also beheld a book that was a scripture for the Jews, bore record of Christ, and went forth to the Gentiles by the Twelve Apostles. Within a short time, however, some of those who had control over the book took "away from the gospel of the Lamb many parts which are plain and most precious" (1 Nephi 13:20–26).

This has been a bone of contention between the Latter-day Saints and many other modern Christians. Most Christians today, and in Joseph's day, believe that the Bible is complete—that it contains everything that God intended, and that no new scriptures should be added. From Joseph's translation of the Book of Mormon, however, we learn that the Bible is not complete and that many important parts are missing. Today's Biblical scholarship sides with Joseph Smith.

The scriptures we have today are the result of actions taken in the second century AD by those who had the power to determine what scriptures they wanted to include in the New Testament. Christian writers at the beginning of the second century had a different Bible than those at the end of that same century.

Clement of Rome—who is generally seen as one of the earliest Christian authors after the New Testament—quotes not only from the Bible we have today, but also quotes from books not in our Bibles as well as scriptural passages that are unknown from any writings that have survived to the present. As John Gee points out, "Clement quotes Moses as saying: 'I am smoke from a vessel,' a quotation that is not found in any known biblical or apocryphal work. Clement further cites a passage from Psalms 28: 'Thou shalt raise me up and I shall acknowledge thee.' This reading of the Psalm, however, is not attested in any extant manuscript."[4]

One passage that he attributes to Ezekiel is not found in our bibles, and the passages he quotes as scripture are not found in any currently known source. In yet other instances, Clement quotes scripture that sometimes vary significantly from what we find in later Biblical manuscripts.

In addition to those texts which have been lost to Christianity, the Bible makes mention of several books which are no longer to be found. A partial list follows: the book of the wars of the Lord (Numbers 21:14); book of Jasher (Joshua 10:13; 2 Samual 1:18); book of Gad the seer (1 Chronicles 29:29); book of Nathan the prophet (1 Chronicles 29:29; 2 Chronicles 9:29); an epistle of Paul to the Corinthians, earlier than our present 1 Corinthians (1 Corinthians 5:9); possibly an earlier epistle to the Ephesians (Ephesians 3:3); and an epistle to the Church at Laodicea (Colossians 4:16).

Dr. Nibley notes that in the recently rediscovered "Epistle of Peter to Jacob 2," Peter is disturbed about the misinterpretation of his words and says so in a letter to James: "They think they are able to interpret my own words better than I can, telling their hearers that they are conveying my very thoughts to them, while the fact is that such things never entered my mind. If they take such outrageous liberties while I am alive, what will they do after I am gone!"[5]

The early Christian Irenaeus claims that the Valentinians changed the scriptures " 'by transferring passages, and dressing them up anew, and making one thing out of another.' " Tertullian, who lived at the end of the second century (and was the first Christian father to write in Latin) claimed there was proof that the scriptures had become " 'adulterated' "—or corrupt. One Christian sect, he notes, "Does not receive certain Scriptures; and whichever of them it does receive, it perverts by means of additions and diminutions, for the accomplishment of it[s] own purpose; and such as it does receive, it receives not in their entirety; but even when it does receive any up to a certain point as entire, it nevertheless perverts even these by the contrivance of diverse Interpretations."[6]

Tertullian charges the Christian leader Marcion with using a "knife, not the pen, since he made such an excision of the Scriptures as suited his own subject matter," and that "Marcion seems to have singled Luke for his mutilating process."[7] Likewise, he accuses the Valentinian Christian sect with taking "away more, and added more, by removing the proper meaning of every particular word, and adding fantastic arrangements of things which have no real existence." He also claims that some writings "wrongly go under Paul's name" but were actually written by a presbyter in Asia.[8]

Dr. Anderson explains that writings of the Apostolic Fathers— Clement of Rome, Ignatius of Antioch, and Polycarp of Smyrna— "are particularly informative of dangerous administrative and doctrinal deviations that occurred twenty to forty years after the Church lost Peter and Paul."[9] Likewise, Professor Welch notes the "significant stir of criticism" which is now "afoot in Christian theology."[10] He cites the words of non-Mormon Thomas Hoffman who says that theoretically, the rediscovery of a lost epistle from an apostle "could still be accepted in the canon." Hoffman also asks why certain books were excluded from the Bible. Why were such books as the Shepherd of Hermas, the First Epistle of Clement, or the Epistle of Barnabas dropped from the canon of the early Church? It's not altogether clear, he laments.[11]

In some instances the very people who were preserving ancient Christian texts were the ones altering them. Rufinus, a fourth-century copyist for example, said that when he copied the works of early Christian writer, Origen, he (and other copyists) would omit those things that they found contrary to their interpretation of scripture as corrupt or interpolations. In instances where Origen was too vague, notes Rufinus, they would add those thing which they felt was necessary.

Similarly, Macarius, who had translated over seventy of Origen's works into Latin, "removed or cleaned up" those things which he found offensive so "that a Latin reader would find nothing in them that disagrees with *our* belief."[12]

Although some early Christians complained about additions, the most common complaint seems to be about deletions—which is typically easier to make than additions. The same problem plagued the Old Testament. As renowned (non-Mormon) Bible scholar Professor Albright puts it, "Our Hebrew text has suffered much more from losses than from glosses."[13] It's interesting, therefore, to recall that Nephi saw many of the precious and plain parts would be taken away.

Of all the surviving copies of New Testament manuscripts, only about 10 percent date before the time of fourth century Emperor Constantine (who forced the various Christian sects to become united), and only one postage stamp-sized document (containing only ten complete words) dates to the second century. As Dr. Gee explains, nearly all surviving New Testament "come after the time period when accusations of textual corruption are rampant."

> Only ten complete words of the New Testament are attested in manuscript form during the time of textual corruption, and not a single one is attested before that time. If we assemble all the manuscripts from the second and third centuries and just note those chapters where even a part of a verse is attested, we find that entire books are missing, including 1–2 Timothy, 1–2 Peter, 2–3 John and Jude. Of the twenty-eight chapters in the gospel of Matthew, there is no manuscript containing even a single verse of sixteen of these chapters before the end of the third century.[14]

With the permanent losses, additions, and alterations to the Word of God, it's no wonder that a restoration was needed to bring back the plain and precious parts of the gospel.

79. A Closed Canon

Most Christendom today believe that the Bible is complete and that no more scripture can be, or should be, added. This belief, however, is contrary to what we now know about the early Christian and Jewish religions. Dr. Nibley cites two well-known biblical scholars, for example who agree with the general position as taught by Joseph Smith: "For the earliest Christians, the apostolic office, the gift of revelation, and the bringing forth of scripture were always regarded as going hand in hand; and, . . . at least as late as AD 200 it was held to be perfectly legitimate 'for someone to add something to the word of the Gospel.' "[15]

80. The Restoration

The great religious reformer and America's first Baptist leader, Roger Williams, lost faith in the churches of his time and said that there was "no regularly-constituted Church on earth, nor any person authorized to administer any Church ordinance; nor could there be, until new apostles were sent by the great Head of the Church, for whose coming he was seeking."[16]

On another occasion he proclaimed, "The Apostasy . . . hath so far corrupted all, that there can be no recovery out of that apostasy until Christ shall send forth new apostles to plant churches anew."[17]

Such a restoration was prophesied in the Bible: "And I saw another angel fly in the midst of heaven, having the everlasting gospel to preach unto them that dwell on the earth, and to every nation, and kindred and tongue, and people" (Revelation 14:6).

Angels do not perform tasks which man can do. But man could not restore the gospel—God was needed to send messengers for the restoration. Paul likewise said, "And he shall send Jesus Christ, which before was preached unto you: Whom the heaven must receive until the times of restitution of all things, which God hath spoken by the mouth of all his holy prophets since the world began" (Acts 3:20–21).

Notice Paul says "restitution," not "reformation" (which is how the Protestants attempted to recover original Church doctrine). The Greek word *apokatastasis,* from which "restitution" is translated, is also translated as "restoration." To restore means to bring back that which was gone; to reform means to improve on something which has gone wrong. Christ would not return to the earth until the restoration of all things. And a restoration would not be necessary unless Christ's Church had been lost.

81. Premortal Existence

In the Pearl of Great Price, we learn that man had a premortal existence in the Spirit World (see Abraham 3:22–23). This is one of the beliefs that distinguish Latter-day Saints from other Christians. In the book of Jeremiah, however, we find a hint at this same doctrine. The Lord, speaking to Jeremiah, said: "Before I formed thee in the belly I knew thee; and before thou camest forth out of the womb I sanctified thee, and I ordained thee a prophet unto the nations" (Jeremiah 1:5).

We also find support for this doctrine in newly discovered Jewish and Christian writings of the Old World. According to one Jewish scholar, for example, in the first few centuries AD: "The belief was current among

Jews that man's soul was independent of his body, existing eternally in the past and in the future. Only for a short, limited time is it placed in the body of a certain human being. All the souls of the world pre-exist in heaven in a kind of spiritual reservoir."[18]

Some of the early Jews believed that premortal souls dwelt in chambers waiting for their turn to descend into a body.[19] In the Book of Enoch—which was once considered to be scripture by some early Jews as well as some early Christians—we read: "And everything which is found in this world has been before, and has passed before him and has been arranged [organized] before Him . . . all the creations of the world which have existed in each generation, before they came into this world, have existed before Him in their *true* form, even all the souls of the children of man have been before they came down to the world, have all been formed before Him in heaven in the very likeness that they have in this world."[20]

82. Council in Heaven

Not only do newly discovered ancient writings speak of man's pre-earth life, but some speak of the heavenly council which was called before the foundation of the world. One book in the Nag Hammadi Library, for example, depicts the council in heaven in similar fashion to the scene given to us by Joseph Smith: "Let us gather an assembly together. Let us visit that creation of his [God]. Let us send someone forth in it. . . . And I [Christ] said these things to the whole multitude of the multitudinous assembly of the rejoicing Majesty. The whole house of the Father of Truth rejoiced that I am the one who is from them. . . . They charged me since I was willing. I came forth to reveal the glory to my kindred and my fellow spirits."[21]

Researcher Eugene Seaich notes that the Jewish Genesis Rabbah "tells how God took counsel with the pre-existent spirits before creating the world. These were the same spirits that comprised the pre-existent Church in the *Shepherd of Hermas* [a writing used by the early Christian Church]."[22] Nibley illustrates that the ancient Jewish and Christian Apocrypha have a lot to say about the "council in heaven and the plan laid down at the foundation of the world. . . . It is not too much to say that the dominant theme of the Thanksgiving Hymns of the Dead Sea Scrolls is an ecstatic contemplation of the wonder of man's participation in heavenly affairs going back to the beginning."[23]

The doctrine of man's premortal existence and his participation in the heavenly council has been found to be so dominant in early Jewish and Christian writings that (non-Mormon) R. H. Charles claims that "all apocalyptic writing conceives of the whole human history as being 'determined from the beginning in the counsels of God.' "[24] Likewise, the world renowned (non-Mormon) Bible scholar William F. Albright has suggested that the use of the plural terms for deity in Genesis 1:26—"Let us make man in our image"—indicates a meeting of the heavenly council to discuss the creation of man.[25] Other scholars have suggested that the *logos* in John may sometimes be translated as *council,* referring to the premortal heavenly council.[26] It's interesting to note that the word *poem* means "creation," referring to the rejoicing the hosts of heaven did at the heavenly council.

Some scholars have recently established that the Hebrew word for *council* or *heavenly council*—and by association, the decree of the council—is *sod* (also spelled sowd). The King James Bible sometimes translates this word as "secret." In Amos 3:7, for example, we read: "Surely the Lord God will do nothing, but he revealeth his *secret* unto his servants the prophets." The Lord reveals the plans—or the "secret" decree—of the council to his prophets. The Hebrew *sowd* was the precursor for the New Testament's Greek *musterion* or "mystery."[27] Accordingly, non-LDS scholar Raymond E. Brown concludes that the background for the Semitic concept of "mysteries" comes from the belief that the prophets gained knowledge about the secret decrees of the heavenly council.[28]

83. Secret Teachings among the Apostles

Some people are troubled that the Latter-day Saints have temples, which are closed to non-members. They argue that Mormons are secretive and that secrecy is not part of Christianity. The recent discoveries shed by biblical scholarship, however, tells another story. John, writing to his friend Gaius, said, "I had many things to write, but I will not with ink and pen write unto thee: But I trust I shall shortly see thee, and we shall speak face to face" (3 John 1:13–14).

Although Jesus often gave sermons that lasted for hours, all of his words in the New Testament can be read in about a half hour. Both the recently discovered Nag Hammadi Library and the rediscovered writings of the early Church Fathers include many quotes that they attribute to Jesus but are not found in our Bible. Take the fifty-three parables of Jesus, for example. Only three interpretations are given in the scriptures; the rest—as noted in the ancient *Apocryphon of James*—were given behind closed doors to a small group of committed believers. This is also hinted at in Christ's words as found in the New Testament:

> He that hath ears, let him hear. And when he was alone, they that were about him with the twelve asked of him the parable.
> And he said unto them, Unto you it is given to know the mystery of the kingdom of God: but unto them that are without, all these things are done in parables: That seeing they may see, and not perceive; and hearing they may hear, and not understand; lest at any time they should be converted, and their sins should be forgiven them. (Mark 4:9–12)

> And the disciples came, and said unto him, Why speakest thou unto them in parables? He answered and said unto them, Because it is given unto you to know the mysteries of the kingdom of heaven, but to them it is not given. (Matthew 13:10–11)

> All these things spake Jesus unto the multitude in parables; and without a parable spake he not unto them: That it might be fulfilled which was spoken by the prophet, saying, I will open my mouth in parables; I will utter things which have been kept secret from the foundation of the world (Matthew 13:34–35)

According to Near Eastern scholar Dr. William Hamblin, many non-Mormon scholars "believe that they can establish that the canonical Gospel of Mark was literally dependent on, and therefore written after, the *Secret Gospel of Mark*."[29] The early orthodox Christian, Clement of Alexandria (AD 150–215), "believed that Jesus taught secret teachings which were not recorded in the New Testament" and he apparently believed that Christ himself taught secret initiation rituals to a select group of followers.[30]

One Catholic scholar believes that the early Christian Eucharist (sacrament) was originally a secret part of the Mysteries and was not preserved in writing. This is what we find in the *Apostolic Constitutions* (an early Christian document). The Eucharist was performed in secret and leaders advised that "the doors be watched, lest any unbelieving or uninitiated person enter."[31]

Non-LDS scholar Elaine Pagels, who has made an in-depth study of the "secret" teachings of the early Christian Church, says that Christ and the Apostles offered "*secret* teaching, known only to the few."[32] As noted in the appendix, the forty-day literature claims to engage those things which Christ taught his disciples after the resurrection. According to early Christian traditions, Christ imparted many important sacred (and secret) teachings to "Peter, James, and John . . . which they in turn transmitted to the others of the Twelve and to the Seventy."[33] Likewise, Clement of Alexandria wrote that

> Mark during Peter's stay in Rome wrote down the acts of the Lord, nevertheless not telling all, nor even hinting at the sacred ones, but selecting those which he thought most useful for the growth of the investigators' faith. When Peter was martyred, Mark came to Alexandria; polishing both his own and Peter's notes, from which by transferring into his first book those things appropriate for those progressing in the testimony. . . . In no way, however, did he betray those things not discussed, nor did he write down the initiatory teaching of the Lord. . . . And when he died he left his compilation at the church which is in Alexandria, where it is kept very safe and secure to this day, being read only to those who are initiated into the great mysteries."[34]

It's also important to understand the terms *sacred* and *profane* in relation to temple worship. To quote professor of Hebrew Bible Dr. Donald W. Parry, "In the Hebrew Bible one of the principal roots from which the English words *sanctuary* and *temple* originate is [a word] which has the basic meaning of 'separation' or 'withdrawal' of sacred entities from profane things. . . . [or] something that is 'holy' or 'withheld from profane use'. . . . Sacred space is temple space, and profane space is chaos. . . . The Latin word *profanum* (English 'profane') literally means 'before' or 'outside' the temple."[35]

Despite the complaint of some critics, Biblical scholarship sides with Joseph Smith—Christ and his Apostles, taught sacred and secret teachings to a select group of initiated individuals.

84. Sacred Vestments

Because Latter-day Saints believe that the temple is sacred, some temple-related issues are not discussed outside of the temple. Other temple issues, however, such as baptism for the dead and the fact that families can be sealed for eternity, can be discussed outside of the temple. One thing that can and can't be discussed is the fact that Mormons believe in special, sacred clothing that should be worn both inside and outside of the temple. Although I won't discuss sacred garments in LDS theology, I will discuss the belief of early Churchmen about sacred vestments being important to exaltation.

Some LDS scholars, for instance, have done extensive research showing that early Christians and Jews wore sacred vestments—or holy garments—that had some interesting significance for believers. Among these ancient texts we find the *Apocalypse of Adam*, the *Combat of Adam and Eve with Satan*, the *Pistis Sophia*, the *Clementine Recognitions*, *Odes of Solomon*, the *Coptic Bartholomew*, various early books of Enoch, the Gospel of Philip, the *Pearl*, and more.

Nibley notes that in one early Christian writing, the Lord—following the resurrection—formed a prayer circle with his male and female disciples. Jesus stood at the altar while his disciples, "clothed in garments of linen" stood around the Savior.[36] Similar writings always speak of the disciples (in these specials settings with the Savior) being "clothed in their garments" or "clothed in white linen." The whiteness of the linen was symbolic of the purity and light of the heavenly garment.

Another early Christian wrote that the street clothes were taken off in the image of "putting of the old man and his works" and after a washing and anointing, they "put on the garment of the Lord Jesus Christ" which he also referred to as garments of "spiritual white."[37] According to many ancient Near Eastern documents, notes Nibley, "One receives the garment always when passing from one stage of existence to another. It marks the condition one is in. To change the garment is to change one's condition, to perform a passage of initiation. Secrecy is important."[38]

Blake Ostler, another LDS scholar, explains

> The ritual action of putting on a sacred *garment* is properly termed an "endowment." The word garment is, in fact, representative of ordinances found in ancient texts. The Greek word [for] "garment," or [for]

"to clothe upon," was used to represent sacramental, baptismal, and sealing ordinances in the *Clementine Recognitions*, an extremely important and ancient Christian (Ebionite) work. The Latin *induere*, meaning "to clothe," and *inducere*, "to lead or initiate," are the roots for our English word *endowment*. All connote temple ordinances.[39]

According to several early Christians and Jews, the sacred nature of the holy garment had a long tradition that dated back to the premortal life. In Genesis we read that after the fall, God made "coats of skins, and clothed" both Adam and Eve (3:21). The Hebrew words for *light* and *skin* are nearly identical, and so a lot of controversy has resulted to what Adam had for a garment. Based on extra-biblical documents, most scholars believe that Adam had a garment of light in his premortal state but lost that garment when he fell. God then provided another garment of skin. This not only likely refers to Adam taking a physical "skin" body, but we learn from other ancient sources that his garment was made of animal skin to protect Adam while he lay exposed in his fallen state. This new garment also served as a reminder of his former garment of premortal glory.[40]

The new garment that Adam received from God also represented Adam's power and authority—just as priestly garments among various religions do today.[41] Satan, these early traditions tell us, was jealous of Adam and longed for his own premortal garment. Attempting to deceive others, he would appear as an angel of light. According to the ancient *Apocalypse of Adam*, Satan—pretending to be God—appeared to Adam. Satan wanted to take Adam's garment and destroy it, but true angels of God intervened.

Satan's desire to take Adam's garment influenced others throughout the ages. These early writings tell us that Adam gave his garment to Enoch. From Enoch it was passed to Methuselah and then to Noah. Ham wanted the power and authority of the garment and stole it from Noah. Eventually, he gave Adam's garment to his son Cush, who finally passed it on to his son Nimrod. Nimrod, the king of Babel, established a false priesthood (believing that he had the power by virtue of his garment) and created the tower of Babel—a false temple that he built to reach heaven (which is what real temples do).

Some traditions claim that Esau (Isaac's oldest son) ambushed and killed Nimrod and took the garment. The garment was then the birth-right which Esau later sold to Jacob.[42] Other traditions, however, claim that the garment was passed on through a righteous lineage directly to Abraham. Ostler explains, "According to the Rabbis, Abraham received the priesthood after the order of Adam and along with it 'a garment of skin which God gave Adam.' This same skin had been handed down as the 'high-priestly robe' directly from Seth to Methuselah, from Noah to Japeth and Shem, and from them to Abraham."[43]

The stories, of course, refer symbolically to the passing of power, or priesthood, to those who were worthy from those who were worthy.

Several of the ancient traditions claim that the garment was marked with the sacred Name. The righteous symbolically put on Christ—and his name—by receiving baptism and the garment. Some of the early Christian documents tell us that the garments were marked with five cuts that had symbolic reference for the initiated.[44] These marks—or tokens—were apparently the same tokens found on the veil of the temple in Jerusalem. Some ancient texts confuse the garment and the veil and use them interchangeably. Ostler observes, "According to Hugo Odeberg, who translated the *Hebrew Enoch,* the veil was marked with 'the secrets of the world's creation and sustenance . . . in short, the innermost Divine secrets.' The purpose of the marks on the garment and the veil was to initiate the recipient into the divine secrets of the universe."[45]

While Adam's earthly garment was given for protection in this world while he lay exposed in his fallen state,[46] so likewise, the garment helped to protect many early Christians from Satan.[47]

Putting on a new garment was not only symbolic off putting of the old man and being clothed in Christ, but it was also symbolic for putting on a resurrected body after symbolic death. In fact, we find that following a person's real demise, the garment was required to return to God. In the *Apocryphon of James,* for example, when the spirit returns to heaven, it will become "as you were first, having clothed yourself, you become the first who will strip himself, and you shall become as you were before removing the garment."[48] Ostler notes that according to Near Eastern traditions:

> In order for the soul to return to the presence of God, certain ordinances are necessary. Among these ordinances are baptism, washings,

anointings, special garments, and signs as seals and passwords to pass by the angels who guard the gate to God's kingdom. In some accounts, one must be married in the Holy of Holies of the temple in order to obtain the highest of three degrees of glory. Thus, the plurality of the heavens is among the most universal of ancient doctrines, with special glories represented by the moon, stars, and sun. Those who could not receive all the necessary ordinances regarding the . . . required knowledge in this life, could receive them beyond the grave.[49]

Some ancient Near Eastern texts claim that in order for the dead to enter God's presence, they must be properly clothed and possess secret knowledge (or sometimes the name of God). As they pass through the seven heavens, their garments become brighter. Ostler quotes the non-Mormon scholar Hugo Odeberg, who writes that the garment of glory "is a necessary condition of entering the highest heavens, God's abode of light. Hence, the garment is also a mark of the holy, celestial nature of its bearer."[50]

Nibley notes that the ancient texts tell us that the garment is required for special protection when visiting other worlds.[51] When the righteous are resurrected and return to God, they are given new garments of glory (or a return of the garment of glory they formerly possessed). This is mentioned both in the ancient literature as well as in the Book of Mormon: "O how great the plan of our God! For . . . the spirit and the body is restored to itself again . . . and their righteousness, being clothed with purity, yea, even with the robe of righteousness" (2 Nephi 9:13–14).

One final interesting note: Hebrew scholar John Tvedtnes points out that anciently, special temple clothing was required to be donned to enter the temple. One piece of attire, however, was always removed—the shoes or sandals. According to Genesis 3:17–18, the ground was cursed because of Adam—removing one's street shoes kept the temple ritually pure from the ground. Shoes are not needed in heaven or in God's presence because there is no cursed ground. According to one ancient source, the angels walk barefoot on flames of fire.[52] It is therefore interesting to note Joseph Smith's description of his visitation from the angel Moroni:

> While I was thus in the act of calling upon God, I discovered a light appearing in my room, which continued to increase until the room was lighter than at noonday, when immediately a personage appeared at my

bedside, standing in the air, for his feet did not touch the floor.

He had on a loose robe of most exquisite whiteness. It was a whiteness beyond anything earthly I had ever seen; nor do I believe that any earthly thing could be made to appear so exceedingly white and brilliant. His hands were naked, and his arms also, a little above the wrist; so, also, were his feet naked, as were his legs, a little above the ankles. (Joseph Smith—History 1:30–31)

85. Salvation for the Dead

Many of the ordinances performed in the temple focus on the salvation of the dead. In John 3:5, Jesus said that unless a man is baptized and receives the Holy Ghost, "he cannot enter into the kingdom of God." "He that believeth and is baptized shall be saved," said the Lord, "but he that believeth not shall be damned" (Mark 16:16). According to most other Christians, when you die you go directly to either heaven or hell. In support of this belief, Luke 23:43 in often cited. Jesus, who was at the time nailed upon the cross, said to the thief at his side, "To day shalt thou be with me in paradise." The word "paradise," however, does not (and cannot) refer to heaven or the dwelling place of God.

The resurrected Christ, after being dead for three days, met Mary Magdalene in the garden and said to her: "Touch me not; for I am not yet ascended to my Father: but go to my brethren, and say unto them, I ascend unto my Father, and your Father: and to my God, and your God" (John 20:17). Although dead for three days, Jesus had not yet ascended to his father. Where, then, had he been? 1 Peter 3:18–20 and 4:6 gives us the answer, although these passages have confused Christian scholars for centuries.

> For Christ also hath once suffered for sins, the just for the unjust, that he might bring us to God, being put to death in the flesh but quickened by the Spirit: By which also he went and preached unto the spirits in prison; Which sometime were disobedient, when once the longsuffering of God waited in the days of Noah, while the ark was a preparing, wherein few, that is, eight souls were saved by water. (1 Peter 3:18–20)

> For, for this cause was the gospel preached also to them that are

dead, that they might be judged according to men in the flesh, but live according to God in the spirit. (1 Peter 4:6)

The early Christians believed that Christ descended into the spirit world following his crucifixion. No special term was applied to this spirit place whereas several vague expressions were used to denote the spirit world as a place for the dead but which was neither heaven nor hell.[53] The Restored Church teaches that during the three days of Christ's death, Jesus visited the spirit world—the world of the dead—and taught the gospel to those righteous spirits who had died before His coming (some of whom lived in the "days of Noah"), after which he organized his missionaries in the spirit world, so they could teach those who had never had the chance to accept the gospel.

In LDS doctrine, there are two temporary abodes within the spirit world. One is reserved for the righteous who have accepted Christ (including his commandments and ordinances), while the other is reserved for those who have not accepted Christ or never had the opportunity to accept Christ. The righteous spirits are organized to help convert those spirits who have not accepted the gospel. As a number of non-LDS scholars acknowledge, this same thing was taught by some of the early Christians.

Nibley points out, for example, that the non-Mormon J.A. Mac-Cullouch gathered a number of examples from ancient literature that Christ preached to the dead in the spirit world.[54] Non-LDS Carl Schmidt, Nibley also points out, believed that the doctrine of salvation for the dead "was the main theme of Christ's teaching" during his ministry to the spirit world.[55] Several of the early Christians also wrote about Christ's spirit-world ministry. Clement of Alexandria, for instance, said that "Christ went down to Hades [spirit world] for no other purpose than to preach the gospel."[56]

In Matthew 16 Jesus asked his disciples who they thought he was. Peter answered that Jesus was "the Christ, the Son of the living God" (v. 16). Jesus was pleased with Peter's answer and explained that "flesh and blood" had not revealed this knowledge to Peter, but the knowledge had come by revelation. Then Jesus said, "Thou art Peter, and upon this rock I will build my church; and the gates of hell shall not prevail against it. And I will give unto thee the keys of the kingdom of heaven:

and whatsoever thou shalt bind on earth shall be bound in heaven: and whatsoever thou shalt loose on earth shall be loosed in heaven" (vv. 18–19).

Some people have thought that this verse means that the Church would be built on Peter, but from the context we can tell that Jesus was saying that his Church was built on revelation. Others have thought that this verse suggests that Satan (which some interpret from the "gates of hell") could not prevail against the Church—that there could be no general apostasy. As we discussed in section 77, however, many of the apostles knew an apostasy was at hand. As non-LDS biblical scholar Adolf von Harnack explains, there are no scriptural passages that refer to the "gates of hell" as the realm of Satan or his hosts. Instead, it refers to gates which hold back the dead from progressing.[57] Before Christ visited the spirit world, the gates of hell separated the dead from the unbaptized dead. Christ had the power, the authority, the "key" to open those gates, and he passed that authority on to Peter. This key allows the spirits who had not yet received the gospel the opportunity to accept or reject Christ and his baptism. Thus Ignatius wrote: "Until Christ came and opened the door [gate], no one, no matter how righteous, could enter the presence of the Father. Only after the resurrection was a common existence with the Father and Jesus Christ possible."[58]

Christ went to preach to the dead so that the dead would have the opportunity to accept the gospel—for "he that believeth not shall be damned" (Mark 16:16). Belief, however, is only part of it. "He that believeth and is *baptized* shall be saved" (Mark 16:16; italics added), and "Except a man be born of the water [baptized] and of the Spirit [receive the gift of the Holy Ghost], he cannot enter into the kingdom of God" (John 3:5). Christ's mission to the dead was to prepare them for these very ordinances.

As the ancient Christian literature shows, Christ's descent to the spirit world emphasizes the fact that his mission in death was simply a continuation of his mission in life, and the spirits in the underworld joined his Church by way of the same ordinances as their mortal descendants.[59] It is also interesting to note that, according to the early Christian writings, not only was John the Baptist born before Christ so he could herald Christ's ministry, but he was also killed by Herod before

Christ's crucifixion "so that he might descend to the lower regions and announce [preach] his [Christ's] coming." John was the forerunner of Christ's mortal ministry, preparing them for the Lord, and likewise he died first "that he might prepare those in hades [the Spirit World] for the gospel; he became the forerunner there, announcing even as he did on this earth, that the Savior was about to come to ransom the spirits of the saints from the hand of death."[60] And how were these Saints to be ransomed? Through the same ordinances which were required of the living—which included baptism.

"Christians," writes one anti-Mormon, "did not and do not now baptize for the dead."[61] The Apostle Paul, while attempting to convince those he was teaching of the reality of the resurrection said: "Else what shall they do which are baptized for the dead, if the dead rise not at all? why are they then baptized for the dead?" (1 Corinthians 15:29).

Most other Churches have not known what to make of this verse, yet the majority of biblical scholars recognize that some of the Corinthians were practicing a proxy baptism in behalf of their deceased friends and relatives.[62] As Nibley explains, according to some of the early Christian literature, the first thing which Christ did upon arrival in the Spirit world was to confer the " 'seal' of baptism upon all to whom he preached in the underworld before they can follow him out of darkness up into his kingdom."[63]

Nibley continued: "In one of the very earliest Christian poems Christ is described as going to the underworld to preach to the dead, 'And the dead say to him, "Open the gate to us!" ' whereupon the Lord, 'heeding their faith,' gives them the seal of baptism. Baptism for the dead, then, was the key to the gates of hell which no church claimed to possess until the nineteenth century, the gates remaining inexorably closed against those very dead of whose salvation the early Christians had been so morally certain."[64]

Clement of Alexandria wrote that "Christ visited, preached to, and baptized the just men of old, both gentiles and Jews, not only those who lived before the coming of the Lord, but also those who were before the coming of the Law . . . such as Abel, Noah, or any such righteous man."[65] As pointed out by the early Christian writers, the spirits of the dead were not actually baptized by water—although there was indeed a baptism of the spirit—but rather the living performed the rite of baptism by proxy in place of those who had died.[66] One Catholic historian claims that in the early Christian Church, the "necessity of Baptism is such that the Apostles and teachers who preached the Gospel had to go down to limbo, there to teach and baptize the just already dead."[67]

In 1945, the late Paul R. Cheesman recorded (with permission) a dialogue with non-Mormon Edgar J. Goodspeed (world renowned expert on early Christian documents) on the subject of baptism for the dead.

> Cheesman: Is the scripture found in 1 Corinthians 15:29 translated properly as found in the King James Translation?
> Goodspeed: Basically, yes.
> Cheesman: Do you believe that baptism for the dead was practiced in Paul's time?
> Goodspeed: Definitely, yes.
> Cheesman: Does the church to which you belong practice it today?
> Goodspeed: No.
> Cheesman: Do you think it should be practiced today?
> Goodspeed: This is the reason why we do not practice it today. We do not know enough about it. If we did, we would practice it.
> Cheesman: May I quote you as a result of this interview?
> Goodspeed: Yes.[68]

86. Degrees of Glory

In 1832, Joseph Smith had a vision wherein he saw that the afterlife was divided into three degrees of glory: the telestial, the terrestrial, and the celestial kingdoms (D&C 76). While most other Christians believe that the souls of the dead go either to heaven or hell, that is not what we find in the scriptures. Jesus, for example, said: "In my Father's house there are many mansions: if it were not so, I would have told you. I go to prepare a place for you" (John 14:2).

Likewise, Paul noted:

> There are also celestial bodies, and bodies terrestrial: but the glory of the celestial is one, and the glory of the terrestrial is another. There is one glory of the sun, and another glory of the moon, and another glory of the stars: for one star differeth from another star in glory. So also is the resurrection of the dead. (1 Corinthians 15:40–42)

I knew a man in Christ above fourteen years ago . . . such an one caught up to the third heaven. (2 Corinthians 12:2)

Christ spoke of many mansions and Paul compared the difference between the glory of the sun, moon, and stars with the different glory of those at the resurrection. Richard Anderson explains, "[Paul] sometimes wrote 'heaven' of the place where God dwells, but he used 'heavens' twice as much. Paul normally used the plural, even though the King James Version sometimes writes the singular for the Greek plural. For Paul, Christ is exalted 'far above all heavens' (Ephesians 4:10). If Christ is literally 'higher than the heavens' (Hebrews 7:26), he is in the highest heaven."[69]

Once, while Jesus was speaking in parables, he told the story of the sower, explaining that what one sows, one reaps: "But other [seeds] fell into good ground, and brought forth fruit, some an hundredfold, some sixtyfold, some thirtyfold. Who hath ears to hear, let him hear" (Matthew 13:8–9).

Commenting on this passage, the very early Christian writer, Irenaeus, wrote:

As the elders say, "Then those who are thought worthy of abode in heaven will go there, others will enjoy the delights of paradise, others will possess the splendor of the city; for everywhere the Saviour will be seen, according as those who see him will be worthy." This is the distinction of the dwelling place of those who bring forth fruit a hundredfold, sixtyfold, and thirty respectively; for some will be taken up into the heavens, others will dwell in paradise, and others will inhabit the city. This is why the Lord said, "In my Father's house are many mansions." For all things are of God, who provides for all a suitable dwelling place.[70]

87. Deification

Joseph Smith taught that we are of the same lineage and race as God. As God's children, we have the potential to reach spiritual maturity and become like him. Most other Christians are shocked or outraged at such a suggestion. But that is exactly what the scriptures tell us. The Psalmist wrote: "Ye are gods; and all of you are children of the most High" (Psalms

82:6). Dr. Keith Norman, who holds a PhD in early Christian studies from Duke University, explains:

> More than once pious Jews tried to stone Jesus when he hinted of his own divinity (John 8:58–59; 10:30–31), and Jesus defended this "blasphemy" on the second occasion by quoting Psalms 82–6: "Is it not written in your law, I said Ye are gods?" (John 10:34). This saying he describes as "The word of God," and furthermore "the scripture cannot be broken" (v. 35). Jesus made no concessions to "human nature" in his expectation of his disciples, and his central statement in the Sermon on the Mount remains the supreme challenge to mankind: "Be ye therefore perfect; *even as your Father in Heaven is perfect.* (Matthew 5:48; italics added).[71]

If we are to be *perfect* as our Father in Heaven is perfect, we must become like our Heavenly Father—otherwise we would be less perfect. "To him that overcometh," said the Lord, "will I grant to sit with me in my throne, even as I also overcame, and am set down with my Father in his throne" (Revelation 3:21). Paul understood that we are literal children of God and that if faithful we, like Christ, would inherit all that God has:

> And if children [of God], then heirs; heirs of God, and joint-heirs with Christ; if so be that we suffer with him, that we may be also glorified together. (Romans 8:17)

> Wherefore thou art no more a servant, but a son; and if a son, then an heir of God through Christ. (Galatians 4:7)

The Greek word *kleronomos,* which is translated above as "heir," is defined by non-Mormon scholars as "a sharer by lot, i.e., an inheritor"[72] and is also used in Hebrews 1:2 where Jesus is "appointed heir of all things, by whom also he made the worlds." Likewise, joint-heir (*sugkleronomos*) means "participant in common—fellow (joint-heir, heir together, heir with)."[73] The righteous, notes the Apostles, will be filled with "all the fullness of God" (Ephesians 3:19) and shall become "partakers of the divine nature" (2 Peter 1:4). If we follow the commandments of God, if we live like Christ, then we will become like Christ, we will become like God for we will inherit all that God has.

Many ancient Christians in the primitive Church understood that we are to follow Christ's example in a literal sense. Thus, Gregory of Nazianus taught: "I may become God to the same extent as He became man."[74] Likewise, the early Christian Irenaeus wrote that Jesus Christ became "what we are, that He might bring us to be even what He is Himself."[75] Clement of Alexander (c. AD 150–215) wrote that Jesus became man so that we might learn "how to become a God." The early Christian Origen wrote:

> And thus the first-born of all creation, who is the first to be with God, and to attract to Himself divinity, is a being of more exalted rank than the other gods beside Him, of whom God is the God, as it is written, "The God of gods, the Lord, hath spoken and called the earth." It was by the offices of the first-born that they became gods, for He drew from God in generous measure that they should be made gods, and He communicated it to them according to His own bounty. The true God, then, is 'The God,' and those who are formed after Him are gods, images, as it were, of Him the prototype.[76]

Likewise, the third century Hippolytus, Bishop of Portus, explained the righteous will become "a companion of the Deity, and a co-heir with Christ, no longer enslaved with lusts or passions, and never again wasted by disease, for thou hast *become God*. . . . Whatever it is consistent with God to impart, these God has promised to bestow upon thee, because thou has *been deified*, and begotten unto immortality."[77]

The early Christian Irenaeus, who was a disciple of Polycarp, a direct disciple of John the Revelator, wrote:

> We were not made gods at our beginning, but first we were made men, then, in the end, gods.
>
> How then will any be a god, if he has not first been made a man? How can any be perfect when he has only lately been made man? How immortal, if he has not in his mortal nature obeyed his maker? For one's duty is first to observe the discipline of man and thereafter to share in the glory of God.
>
> Our Lord Jesus Christ, the Word of God, of his boundless love, became what we are that he might make us what he himself is.[78]

Basil of Caesaria, notes Phillip Barlow, "preached that the Holy Spirit aids man in 'being made like to God—and highest of all, being made God.'" Even Athanasius, the champion defender of the "Trinity" doctrine formed at Nicea, taught that the Lord "assumed humanity that we might become God."[79]

Clement of Alexandria explained that the righteous are "given their reward and their honors. . . . because of their close intimacy with the Lord there awaits them a restoration to eternal contemplation; and they have received the title of 'gods' since they are destined to be enthroned with the other 'gods' who are ranked next below the savior."[80]

Even as late as the early part of the fourth century, Athanasius said that Christ "was made man that we might be made God."[81] The early Christian writings on deification are so common that non-Mormon scholar G.L. Prestige claimed that the Primitive Christian Church "taught that the destiny of man was to become like God, and even to become deified."[82]

88. Word of Wisdom

In the winter of 1833, Joseph organized the "School of the Prophets" wherein priesthood holders would meet for discussion and learning. Joseph seemed disturbed by the fact that each meeting was held in a cloud of smoke, and his wife, Emma, complained about having to clean the room of spit from chewing tobacco. Concerned over the matter, Joseph turned to the Lord and received a revelation now known as the Word of Wisdom (see D&C 89). The Word of Wisdom contains a plan for healthy living by proscribing certain vices, such as tobacco, alcohol, and "hot drinks" (which have been defined by the Church as coffee and tea), while advising the consumption of other foods such as fruits, vegetables, and grains.

When this revelation was initially disclosed, the Lord said that it was given by way of wisdom, "not by commandment or constraint" (v. 2). Joseph F. Smith explains that if the revelation had been given as a commandment in Joseph Smith's day, "it would have brought every man [and woman] addicted to the use of these noxious things under condemnation; so the Lord was merciful and gave them a chance to overcome, before He brought them under the law."[83]

Obedience to the principles contained in the Word of Wisdom were urged since the days of Joseph Smith, and by the 1920s, under inspiration, the Church regarded the Word of Wisdom as a binding principle and insisted on obedience by restraining from the use of alcoholic beverages, tobacco, coffee, and tea.

In 1833, when this revelation was made, the science and medicine of the times were not in a position which could verify the harmful effects of these substances on the body. Some other groups, both religious and nonreligious, refrained from the use of tobacco for one reason or another, and drunkenness has always been frowned upon, but in general the Word of Wisdom was far ahead of its day. Even as late as 1964, one anti-Mormon wrote: "Recent evidence linking cigarette smoking with lung cancer and other disorders confirms the wisdom of the Word of Wisdom for Mormon believers. Available evidence seems to indict only the cigarette; those who have been smoking pipes and cigars do not seem to be in much danger from lung cancer. At the time the revelation was given—1833—the usual form in which tobacco was used was in pipes or as snuff or chew."[84]

Tobacco

The above critic implies that because cigarettes were not common in 1833, and since (according to 1964 evidence) pipes, cigars, snuff, and chewing tobacco didn't cause cancer or disorders, then Joseph Smith was wrong concerning the Word of Wisdom. How far we have come. People who smoke pipes and cigars don't usually inhale as deeply and are therefore not exposed to as much smoke from the tobacco as are those who smoke cigarettes; therefore, heart attacks and lung cancer are considerably lower among those who smoke pipes and cigars. Cancer of the larynx, esophagus, and mouth, however, are practically equal to that of cigarette smokers. Recent studies on chewing tobacco have shown distinct links to mouth and lip cancer.[85] Besides, cigarette smoking may not have been as popular in Joseph Smith's day, but it certainly is in our day, and the Word of Wisdom is meant for our counsel probably more than it was for those in the days of Joseph Smith.

According to a 1986 statement by Dr. James Mason, director of the Center of Disease Control in Atlanta, cigarette smoking is the "single most important cause of disease and premature death." Tobacco, he notes, "kills thirteen times as many Americans as hard drugs do, and eight times as many as automobile accidents." In 1986, it was estimated that tobacco killed 2.5 million people annually. Smokeless tobacco—such as snuff and chew—are "linked to oral, pharyngeal, and laryngeal cancer."[86]

Those who don't smoke but live with smokers are "three times more likely to die of lung cancer than those not exposed."[87] Former Surgeon General C.E. Koop noted his concern over passive smoke. According to his research reports, children of families with parents who smoke are more likely to be hospitalized with pneumonia or bronchitis than children whose parents do not smoke.[88]

Reports claim that tobacco kills more adults in the United States than any other preventable cause of death: "More deaths are caused each year by tobacco use than by all deaths from human immunodeficiency virus (HIV), illegal drug use, alcohol use, motor vehicle injuries, suicides, and murders combined."[89]

Alcohol

Alcohol consumption, like smoking, is a vice that has caused needless deaths worldwide. Not only has drinking been the cause of automobile-related deaths, but heavy consumption has also been linked to cancers of the mouth, esophagus, and pharynx.[90]

Critics of the Word of Wisdom have sometimes cited studies which indicate that the consumption of small quantities of alcohol—especially wine—can be healthy. While there may be some truth to this claim, the problem lies in the fact that most people have little self-control, especially with something so potentially addictive as alcohol. Too many people have problems with moderation. Drinking small quantities of alcohol on limited occasions can lead to addiction and future problems. According to a 1987 Gallup Poll, for instance, about one out of five American homes had an immediate family member who had sought professional help in overcoming a drinking problem.[91]

Besides, it is not so clear that alcohol has the positive effects touted by some critics. As Dr. Charles S. Lieber explains,

> Claims that wine is healthier than other alcoholic beverages have not been consistently corroborated. . . . A drink a day does not keep the doctor away. This is what we should be telling patients who ask if they

should start having a drink every day because they heard it lowers the risk of heart attack or stroke.

. . . In short, an evidence-based approach to health care does not support advising patients to start drinking for therapeutic purposes, especially when we already have effective, evidence-based ways to lower cardiovascular risk. Even if moderate drinking turns out to be beneficial in some people, the risk of developing alcohol abuse outweighs any potential cardiovascular benefits.[92]

Coffee and Tea

The big problem with coffee and tea—especially coffee in the United States—is that many coffee consumers drink several cups a day:

[The] per capita consumption of coffee in America is three-and-one half cups per day, an average intake of from 350 to 525 mg. of caffeine. Even 50 to 200 mg. of caffeine per day is considered medically a physiologic dose that may produce side effects. Two major pharmacology medical school texts refer to doses of caffeine exceeding 250 mg. as significant. So, two cups of coffee or tea contain a clinically significant dose of this drug.[93]

While high doses of caffeine in any form can potentially be harmful, some research shows that even decaffeinated coffee and tea is linked to certain disorders. In one recent study coffee—not caffeine—was linked to lung cancer. Dr. Leonard Schuman, an epidemiologist at the University of Minnesota said that "this is the first time that coffee has been implicated by itself."[94]

The Wholesome Word of Wisdom

Thus far we have focused on the negative things contained within the Word of Wisdom. There are also, however, several items which are encouraged for consumption. The Lord stresses the consumption of fruits, vegetables, grains, and the sparing use of meats. These are areas in which the Latter-day Saints could use some improvement.

The use of fruits and vegetables has been known to promote good health for many years. In recent years, however, several important medical studies have shown the remarkable benefits of diets which are high in grain, or bran. Several studies indicate that high bran diets can actually help prevent several types of cancer. Many cereal and bread manufacturers have picked up on these studies and have used these findings to promote their products. Nearly every grocery store carries several brands of cereal, breads, or health foods which advertise the fact that their product contains bran or fiber, which has proven to be beneficial to a healthy diet. Some grocery stores even have entire health food sections full of these high-fiber products.

As for the use of meat, recent research suggests that too much red meat can be unhealthy due to the high content of fat and cholesterol. The Word of Wisdom, however, does not say to forego meat completely, but only to use it sparingly. Meat is an excellent source of protein. While dairy products and eggs are high in protein as well, many adults cannot properly digest the lactose in milk, and eggs are also high in cholesterol. Grains contain very little protein, and although some vegetables contain adequate amounts of protein, many other vegetables and most fruits do not. Besides, meat also contains several members of the vitamin B group, including thiamin, niacin, riboflavin, pantothenic acid, and pyridoxine. Meat used sparingly is not only filling and tasty, but healthy as well. It is interesting to note that, according to research, vegetarian Seventh-day Adventists (SDAs neither smoke nor drink) have lower colon cancer rates than non-vegetarian SDAs, but Mormon rates are even lower despite the consumption of meat.[95]

The Lord included a rough, although very accurate, sketch of things which should and should not be contained in our diets. Dr. James Mason, formerly the Assistant Secretary for Health in the Department of Health and Human Services, believes that Section 89 of the Doctrine and Covenants encompasses everything we now know about nutrition.[96]

By Their Fruits

The Word of Wisdom was given for our happiness, not as a punishment. We lose our agency when we partake of harmful substances and become addicted to them. The Lord offered a way to know the difference between true prophets and false prophets: "Ye shall know them by their fruits. Do men gather grapes of thorns, or figs of thistles? Even so every good tree bringeth forth good fruit; but a corrupt tree bringeth forth evil fruit. A good tree cannot bring forth evil fruit, neither can a corrupt tree bringeth forth good fruit. Every tree that bringeth not forth good fruit is hewn down, and cast into the fire. Wherefore by their fruits ye shall know them" (Matthew 7:16–20).

Several studies have been done comparing Mormon health statistics with non-Mormon health statistics. A study in 1973, for example, found:

> In heavily Mormon Utah County, the cancer death rate for men is 35 percent below the national average; for women it's 28 percent less than in the United States as a whole.
>
> The State of Utah, nearly three-fourths Mormon, has the lowest cancer death rate by far of any state in the United States—27 percent lower for men and 26 percent lower for women.
>
> In California, where there are no complicating environmental differences—such as clean Rocky Mountain air—and where [Dr. James] Enstrom directly compared the deaths of Mormons and non-Mormons from cancer over a three-year period [in the California study noted above], the deaths of Mormons are *21 percent less* for women and nearly *one-third less* for men.
>
> Particularly low for Mormons in all three regions are deaths from cancer of the mouth, throat, stomach, lung, colon, rectum and bladder.[97]

While the researchers attribute much of the Mormon's health statistics to the Word of Wisdom, they also found that there were other factors in Mormon health statistics that are hard to explain by diet: "Epidemiologist Dr. Joseph Lyon is particularly perplexed over the Mormon's low rates of cancer of the cervix, breast and stomach (only 40 percent of the national average). 'No one has ever demonstrated,' [Lyon said], 'that these types of malignancies are associated with diet, tobacco, alcohol or any external or environmental cause.' "[98]

While this study found that the Mormon rate for cancers related to smoking and drinking are extremely low, they also found low incidence of diseases such as "diabetes, and cancers of the stomach, colon, breast, kidney, and the lymph glands, none of which have ever been associated with smoking or drinking."[99]

Another study conducted in Alameda County in the East San Francisco Bay area, reviewed the health statistics of 111 practicing Mormons among nearly 7,000 adults in that county. This study found that Mormons in the sample area had "a mortality rate only 55 percent as great as the total sample in that county."[100] Mormons also had "low rates . . . for cancer of the stomach, colon, breast, kidney, and other sites that have never before been clearly related to factors such as smoking."[101]

Dr. Enstrom, who worked on the California study, claims that the "remaining life expectancy for active Mormon men at age 35 is about 44 years, which compares with 36.5 years for all U.S. white males and 39.6 years for U.S. white males who never smoked cigarettes."[102] Government studies show that "Utah death rates for the two leading causes of death, heart disease and cancer, are more than 40 percent lower than U.S. rates."[103]

When the Word of Wisdom was first revealed, the health benefits that could have been attained from strict observance were minimal. Life expectancy was thirty-five years and by 1900 was still less than fifty years—less than that of underdeveloped countries today.[104] While the Word of Wisdom would have extended the lives of nineteenth-century adult Latter-day Saints, most Saints (and non-members) died in either infancy or before they would have reached an age when the Word of Wisdom's preventive effects (cancer, heart disease, and so forth) would have any real impact.[105] The Lord, of course, knew that the time would come when adherence to the Word of Wisdom would impact the life expectancy and health of the Saints. Considering the length of time it took for the Saints to comprehend the significance of the Word of Wisdom and wean themselves from the addictive elements that it proscribed, it's interesting that by the time this realization was made, the health value of the revelation was real. As Lester Bush wrote:

> Whatever merit or function the Word of Wisdom had for the nineteenth century Mormons, in retrospect we know that circumstances changed around the turn of the century in such a way that its guidelines would unquestionably promote better physical health (i.e., there was more cigarette smoking, and less serious infectious disease). That this development—the implications of which were not apparent to the medical scientists for decades—coincided with a decision by the church leadership to require firm adherence to the Word of Wisdom is quite remarkable. It may well represent their most demonstrably prescient insight to date in helping assure that the "destroying angel" of disease will "pass us by."[106]

While the healthy benefits of the Word of Wisdom are seen in longer lives and less cancer among the Saints, the primary advantage of the Word of Wisdom is spiritual. Abstinence from harmful substances teaches us how to curb appetites and helps us avoid situations where we are unable to use our full mental faculties. Alcohol, for example, can impair our judgments.

Last, the Word of Wisdom is a principal of unity. Throughout history, God's people have had protocols which kept them from the world while still being in the world. Circumcision and the Mosaic Law all, in part, helped distinguish a people who were committed to God's law; it helped separate them from the worldliness around them. Non-observance or observance of the Word of Wisdom often reflects one's commitment to God as well as approaches to other commandments or even a general lifestyle. Adherence to the Word of Wisdom is often a mark of a committed Latter-day Saint.

89. Fruits of Education

Statistics also favor Utah when it comes to education. Utah, for example, is tied for second place in "producing people listed in *Leaders in Education*," and is first "as the birthplace of people listed in *American Men of Science*."[107] Typically, LDS adults in the United States "are much more likely to have had post-high school education" than other adults in the United States.[108]

The success factor of colleges and universities is indicated in a productivity index. In 1974, Kenneth Hardy, writing for *Science* magazine observed, "The most productive state is Utah, which is first in productivity for all fields combined in all time periods. . . . Compared to other states in its region, it is deviantly productive. This result seems clearly to be due to the influence of Mormon values."[109]

Another study has concluded that the average productivity index for Brigham Young University, Utah State University, and the University of Utah, is 50 percent higher than Massachusetts Institute of Technology, and over twice the average productivity index of Stanford and Yale combined.[110]

Some studies also suggest that, in unique contrast to most other Christian faiths, higher education among LDS seems to contribute to Latter-day Saints religiosity. Studies conducted of several mainline Protestant groups, for example, show that the religiosity of members declined as education increased. Most people tend to move away from certain religious beliefs as their learning in the secular world increases. All studies indicate that education has an overwhelmingly "negative effect" on religiosity. It seems that the "the higher the level of education, the higher the probability that their respondents would have apostatized from the church." Increased "education tends both to expand one's horizons and increase exposure to counter-cultural values." "In other words," notes one researcher, "poorly grounded religious beliefs have simply been unable to stand in the face of challenges generated by modern science and higher education."[111] This is generally not the case, however, with Latter-day Saints.

A study of Mormons that included the college-educated and the non-college-educated reveals that "those with post-bachelor's degrees are, on the average, more religious than those who never attended college." College-educated Latter-day Saints, "both as a group and by specific level of education, were, on the average, *more religiously involved* than noncollege educated Latter-day Saints."[112] In direct contrast to the negative effect associated with education and religion for other groups, studies of Latter-day Saints have shown "a strong positive relationship between level of education and religiosity. . . . Whether we are talking about personal value placed on religious beliefs, attendance at church, financial contributions, frequency of personal prayer, or frequency of gospel study, the impact of increased education among Latter-day Saints is positive. . . . The secularizing influence of higher education simply doesn't seem to hold for Latter-day Saints."[113]

NOTES

1. Richard Lloyd Anderson, "Clement, Ignatius, and Polycarp: Three Bishops Between the Apostles and Apostasy," *Ensign,* Aug. 1976, 51–52.
2. "Greek Dictionary of the New Testament," *Interlinear Greek-English New Testament* (Grand Rapids, MI: Baker Book House, 1981), 15.
3. Anderson, "Clement, Ignatius, and Polycarp: Three Bishops Between the Apostles and Apostasy," 55.

4. John Gee, "The Corruption of Scripture in the Second Century," at http://www.fairlds.org/FAIR_Conferences/1999_Corruption_of_Scripture_in_the_Second_Century.html (accessed 5 July 2008).

5. Quoted in Hugh Nibley, "Prophets and Preachers," *The World and the Prophets* (Salt Lake City, UT: Deseret Book; Provo, UT: FARMS, 1987), 28.

6. Gee, "The Corruption of Scripture in the Second Century."

7. Ibid.

8. Ibid.

9. Anderson, "Clement, Ignatius, and Polycarp: Three Bishops Between the Apostles and Apostasy," 51.

10. John W. Welch, "The Plain and Precious Parts," *Reexploring the Book of Mormon,* 39.

11. Ibid.

12. Gee, "The Corruption of Scripture in the Second Century."

13. Nibley, *Since Cumorah,* 26.

14. Gee, "The Corruption of Scripture in the Second Century."

15. Hugh Nibley, "The Prophets and the Scripture," *The World and the Prophets,* 202.

16. Vestal and Wallace, *The Firm Foundation of Mormonism,* 235.

17. Ibid.

18. Ibid., 229.

19. Eugene Seaich, *Ancient Texts and Mormonism* (Murray, UT: Sounds of Zion, 1983), 32.

20. Nibley, "A Strange Thing in the Land: The Return of the Book of Enoch," *Enoch the Prophet,* 242.

21. *Second Treatise of the Great Seth,* translated by Roger A. Bullard and Joseph A. Gibbons at http://www.gnosis.org/naghamm/2seth.html (accessed 6 July 2008).

22. Seaich, *Ancient Texts,* 37.

23. Hugh W. Nibley, *Nibley on the Timely and the Timeless* (Provo, UT: BYU Religious Studies Center, 1978), 27–28.

24. Nibley, *An Approach to the Book of Mormon,* 160.

25. Seaich, *Ancient Texts and Mormonism,* 36–37.

26. Nibley, *Nibley on the Timely and the Timeless,* 33.

27. Eugene Seaich, *Mormonism, the Dead Sea Scrolls, and the Nag Hammadi Texts* (Murray, UT: Sounds of Zion, 1980), iv.

28. John W. Welch, "Lehi's Council Vision and the Mysteries of God," *Reexploring the Book of Mormon,* 24.

29. William J. Hamblin, "Aspects of an Early Christian Initiation Ritual," *By Study and Also By Faith,* 2 vols., eds., John M. Lundquist and Stephen D. Ricks (Salt Lake City, UT: Deseret Book; Provo: FARMS, 1990), 1:206.

30. Ibid., 208, 210.

31. Ibid., 205.

32. Elaine Pagels, *The Gnostic Gospels* (New York: Vintage Books, 1981), 16.

33. Nibley, *Since Cumorah,* 82.

34. Gee, "The Corruption of Scripture in the Second Century."

35. Donald W. Parry, "Demarcation between Sacred Space and Profane Space: The Temple of Herod Model," *Temples of the Ancient World,* ed., Donald W. Parry (Salt Lake City, UT: Deseret Book; Provo, UT: FARMS, 1994), 416.

36. Hugh Nibley, "Sacred Vestments," *Temple and Cosmos,* ed., Don E. Norton (Salt Lake City, UT: Deseret Book; Provo: FARMS, 1992), 96.

37. Ibid., 97.

38. Ibid., 123.

39. Blake Ostler, "Clothed Upon: A Unique Aspect of Christian Antiquity," *BYU Studies* (1981) 22:1, 31.

40. Stephen D. Ricks, "The Garment of Adam in Jewish, Muslim, and Christian Tradition," *Temples of the Ancient World,* 706–708.

41. Ibid., 710–12.

42. Nibley, *Lehi in the Desert,* 170.

43. Ostler, "Clothed Upon: A Unique Aspect of Christian Antiquity," 37.

44. Nibley, "Sacred Vestments," *Temple and Cosmos,* 107–108.

45. Ostler, "Clothed Upon: A Unique Aspect of Christian Antiquity," 34.

46. Nibley, "Sacred Vestments," 124.

47. John A. Tvedtnes, "Priestly Clothing in Bible Time," *Temples in the Ancient World,* 661.

48. Ostler, "Clothed Upon: A Unique Aspect of Christian Antiquity," 5.

49. Ibid.

50. Ibid., 7.

51. Nibley, "Sacred Vestments," *Temple and Cosmos,* 124.

52. Tvedtnes, "Priestly Clothing in Bible Time," 671.

53. Hugh Nibley, "Baptism for the Dead in Ancient Times," *Mormonism and Early Christianity* (Salt Lake City, UT: Deseret Book; Provo, UT: FARMS, 1987), 115.

54. Hugh Nibley, "Christ Among the Ruins," Ensign (July 1983), 17.

55. Nibley, "Baptism for the Dead in Ancient Times," 100.

56. Ibid., 118.

57. Ibid., 105–106, 108.

58. Ibid., 116.

59. Ibid., 119.

60. Ibid., 121.

61. Floyd C. McElveen, *The Mormon Illusion* (Ventura, CA: Regal Books, 1977), 116.

62. Richard L. Anderson, *Understanding Paul* (Salt Lake City, UT: Deseret Book, 1983), 404.

63. Nibley, "Christ Among the Ruins," 18.

64. Nibley, "Baptism for the Dead in Ancient Times," 106.

65. Ibid., 122–23.

66. Ibid., 123–24.

67. Vestal and Wallace, *The Firm Foundation of Mormonism*, 231.

68. Anderson, *Understanding Paul,* 413.

69. Ibid., 143.

70. *Early Christian Fathers,* ed., Cyril C. Richardson (New York: Macmillan Publishing, 1970), 396.

71. Keith Norman, "Divinization: The Forgotten Teaching of Early Christianity," *Sunstone* (Winter 1975): 15–16.

72. "Greek Dictionary of the New Testament," 42.

73. Ibid., 67.

74. Philip Barlow, "Unorthodox Orthodoxy: The Idea of Deification in Christian Theology," *Sunstone* (September/October 1983): 15.

75. James L. Barker, *Apostasy from the Divine Church* (Salt Lake City, UT: Bookcraft, 1960), 70.

76. Quoted in "Deification of Man," at http://en.fairmormon.org/Deification_of_man#Origen_.28ca._AD_185-251.29 (accessed 6 July 2008).

77. Seaich, *Ancient Texts and Mormonism,* 45.

78. Quoted in "Deification of Man," at http://en.fairmormon.org/Deification_of_man#Irenaeus_.28ca._AD_115-202.29 (accessed 7 July 2008).

79. Philip Barlow, "Unorthodox Orthodoxy: The Idea of Deification in Christian Theology," 15.

80. Quoted in Martin, Tanner, Review of Melodie Moench Charles, "Book of Mormon Christology," *FARMS Review* 7, no. 2 (1995): 19 n. 26.

81. Norman, "Divinization: The Forgotten Teaching of Early Christianity," 17.

82. Quoted in "Deification of Man," at http://en.fairmormon.org/Deification_of_man#Modern_Christian_exegesis (accessed 6 July 2008).

83. Leonard J. Arrington, "I Have a Question," *Ensign,* Apr. 1977, 32.

84. Whalen, *The Latter-day Saints in the Modern Day World,* 224.

85. Porter Skinner, "Effect of Tobacco Use Extends Throughout Body, Research Finds," *Colorado Springs Gazette Telegraph,* July 15, 1984.

86. Dr. James Mason, "I Have a Question," *Ensign,* Sept. 1986, 59–61.

87. Ibid.

88. Irvin Molotsky, "Surgeon General Links Smoking to Lung Disease in Nonsmokers," *The New York Times* (24 May 1984), at http://query.nytimes.com/gst/fullpage.html?res=9403E7DE143BF937A15756C0A962948260&sec=health&spon=&pagewanted=all (accessed 3 July 2008).

89. "Tobacco Related Mortality," Center for Disease Control and Prevention, at http://www.cdc.gov/tobacco/data_statistics/Factsheets/tobacco_related_mortality.htm (accessed 3 July 2008).

90. "Alcohol and Cancer," at http://alcoholism.about.com/cs/alerts/l/blnaa21.htm (accessed 3 July 2008).

91. Robin Room, "Cultural Changes in Drinking and Trends in Alcohol Problems Indicators: Recent U.S. Experience," *Alcohol: Drinking Practices and Problems,* eds., Walter B. Clark and Michael E. Hilton (State University of New York Press, 1991), 152, at http://books.google.com/books?id=fh0FCgweAt0C&pg=PA152&lpg=PA152&dq=1987+gallup+poll+alcohol+problems&source=web&ots=Dw7208dk4c&sig=ZvF47t9we7J-Hy4yfzcQ_JFKCLA&hl=en&sa=X&oi=book_result&resnum=1&ct=result (accessed 3 July 2008).

92. Charles S. Lieber, "Alcohol and Health: A Drink a Day Won't Keep the Doctor Away," *The Globe* (2004) at http://www.ias.org.uk/resources/publications/theglobe/globe200401-02/gl200401-02_p37.html (accessed 3 July 2008).

93. Clifford Stratton, "The Xanthines: Coffee, Cola, Cocoa, and Tea," *BYU Studies,* 20, no. 4 (Summer 1980): 372.

94. "Study Ties Cancer to Coffee," *Colorado Springs Gazette Telegraph,* June 23, 1985.

95. Kristen Rogers, "How Healthy Are We?" *This People* (Fall 1989), 14.

96. Ibid.

97. Bill Davidson, "What Can We Learn About Health From the Mormons?" *Family Circle* (January 1976), 78.

98. Ibid.

99. Ibid., 80.

100. "Health Statistics Favor Mormons," *Ensign,* July 1975, 63.

101. Ibid.

102. Vestal and Wallace, *The Firm Foundation of Mormonism,* 241.

103. *Utah in Demographic Perspective,* eds. Thomas K. Martin, Tim B. Heaton, and Stephen J. Bahr (Salt Lake City, UT: Signature Books, 1986), 59.

104. Lester E. Bush Jr., "The Word of Wisdom in Early Nineteenth Century Perspective," *Dialogue: A Journal of Mormon Thought* 14, no. 3 (Autumn 1981): 59.

105. Ibid.

106. Ibid., 60

107. Gerald Scott, "Effects of College Education on the Religious Involvement of Latter day Saints," *BYU Studies* 24, no. 1 (Winter 1984): 44.

108. Howard M. Bahr and Renata Tonks Forste, "Toward a Social Science of Contemporary Mormondom," *BYU Studies* 26, no. 1 (Winter 1986): 92.

109. Kenneth R. Hardy, "Social Origins of American Scientists and Scholars," *Science,* August 1974, 500.

110. Mark W. Cannon, "Mormons in the Executive Suite," *Dialogue: A Journal of Mormon Thought* 3, no. 3 (Autumn 1968): 98.

111. Stan L. Albrecht, "The Consequential Dimension of Mormon Religiosity," *BYU Studies* 29, no. 2 (Spring 1989): 100.

112. Gerald Scott, "Effects of College Education on the Religious Involvement of Latter day Saints," 51; emphasis added

113. Albrecht, "The Consequential Dimension of Mormon Religiosity," 103.

CONCLUSION

*T*he only sure way of knowing if Joseph Smith was a prophet of God, if the Book of Mormon is true, or if God exists and Jesus is the Christ, is by the power of the Spirit. Nevertheless, we can take comfort in knowing that our spiritual convictions have support from the secular world. Since Joseph Smith's day, the world has enjoyed the advances of history, archaeology (in both the Old and New Worlds), and the discovery (or rediscovery) of hitherto forgotten ancient Jewish and Christian texts.

While we can't test the Spirit under a microscope or with a measuring tape, or with calipers, we can compare the works that Joseph was instrumental in bringing forth with what we currently know about the ancient world and early Christianity. The more we learn, the more we find that unique LDS scriptures are consistent with traditions, geography, and the culture from the times and locations for which they claim to have derived. We also find that LDS doctrines accurately reflect many of the things that were once taught by Jesus and his closest disciples.

Scholarly evidences that support the prophetic claims and restorations brought forth by Joseph Smith should fortify a member's testimony and should give curious and questioning hearts a reason to seek the Lord for a confirming spiritual witness.

Appendix

Primer on Ancient Documents

The Church of Jesus Christ of Latter-day Saints claims to be the restored Church; therefore, many of its supposedly "unique" doctrines are actually restored doctrines which had previously been taught by the Lord's Church. This section will look at those ancient writings which shed light on the teachings and beliefs of the early Jews and Christianity. It's also important to note that most of these texts lay unnoticed, unstudied, or unknown until the last seventy-five years.

The Dead Sea Scrolls

Probably the most famous of the newly found writings are the Dead Sea Scrolls, so named because they were found in the caves of Qumran, near the shores of the Dead Sea. While searching for a lost goat, two young Arab boys began throwing stones into caves when they heard the sound of breaking pottery. Investigating, they found some earthen jars that contained seven parchment manuscripts, wrapped in linen, and covered with wax.[1]

At first, the Arabs thought about burning the scrolls as firewood (as they had done in the past) but decided instead to sell them on the black market in Bethlehem. Initially, they were unable to find a buyer. Finally, one shopkeeper had a change of heart and purchased the scrolls. Unable to read the script, the shopkeeper took the scrolls to a Catholic scholar who immediately recognized the worth of the parchment and purchased the manuscripts. Sometime later, this same scholar sold the scrolls to the Israel Government for $250,000.[2]

Following the discovery of these first seven scrolls, the hunt was on for more manuscripts. It was soon discovered that over forty caves contained preserved manuscripts among which we find numerous non-biblical records and all Old Testament books with the exception of Esther.

The exciting thing about the scrolls is that they date from about 200 BC (or earlier) to about AD 65 and therefore, shed light on Christian origins as well as ancient Jewish theology.

Apostolic Fathers

Today, when scholars attempt to reconstruct the teachings of the Primitive Christian Church, they often appeal to the writings of early Christians, bishops, theologians, and historians. These writings, like the Dead Sea Scrolls, were mostly unknown or unavailable during Joseph Smith's lifetime. Following the death of the Twelve Apostles, some faithful bishops of the early Church wrote letters of advice and counsel exhorting members of the Church to live Christlike lives. These men lived during, or shortly after, the time of the Apostles, and several gave their lives for the truth. Their writings reflect the closest teachings to those of the apostles and the Primitive Church prior to the Apostasy.[3]

Clement of Rome, for instance, was praised by Paul as being recorded in "the book of life" (Philippians 4:3) and was a contemporary of the late apostles and says that they were of his "own generation."[4] In addition to the Apostolic Fathers, we also have the writings of early church historians such as Eusebius, bishop of Caesarea, Sozomen, Lactantius, Rufinus, and Flavius Josephus.

While these early Christians had early insight into the Church, that doesn't mean that we should consider everything these men taught as accurate doctrine as revealed by Christ and the Twelve Apostles. In most cases they simply voiced their own knowledge, as well as their own opinions and conjectures. They freely admitted that they didn't have all the answers—they were not apostles, and they knew it. Their writings, however, hold merit because of their close proximity to the lifetime of the apostles.

While some of these authors were not far removed from the days of the apostles, others lived when the influence of the Greek schools of philosophy were in their heyday. Clement of Alexandria and Origen, for instance, were both defenders of philosophy—and we find this in some of their writings. The errors in their writings, however, do not negate the value they serve in providing for us a more accurate picture of what the early Christians believed during the life of the apostles, and what the Primitive Church believed after the death of the apostles.

Nag Hammadi

In 1945, a Christian Library was discovered which was buried in very much the same way as the Dead Sea Scrolls. Muhammad Ali al Samman and his brothers were digging for fertilizing soil in the village of Chenoboskion (near Nag Hammadi, Egypt) when they struck a large earthen jar. At first they were afraid to break open the jar, for they feared it might contain a spirit. After considering that it might contain treasures, however, they smashed the jar and discovered thirteen leather bound books containing over one thousand pages of papyri. Later their mother burned as kindling in the oven some of the papyrus pages which had fallen out of the books. Like the Dead Sea Scrolls, the leather books were initially sold on the black market for about one dollar. In 1952, the Egyptian government purchased the books for about $17,000.[5]

Under the fourth century ruler of Emperor Constantine, the views and books deemed controversial were banned. Bishops who did not agree with Constantine's views were also banned; their property was seized, and any controversial books in their possession were denounced as heretical and burned. Apparently, someone in Upper Egypt hid a number of banned books in a jar where they remained buried for almost sixteen hundred years.[6]

Most of the fifty-two papyrus volumes, bound in these thirteen books, date before the fourth century AD. Several of the manuscripts claim to come from the apostles themselves. There are writings that claim to come from Philip, Thomas, John, Peter, and James (the brother of Jesus). Some writings claim to be associated with ancient patriarchs, such as Adam, Seth, Shem, and Melchizedek,[7] while other writings purport to record the sayings of Jesus as well as secret conversations between Jesus and his disciples following his resurrection.

In addition to the official Nag Hammadi Library, other ancient texts have also turned up in Egypt, including the Gospel of the Twelve Apostles which the early Christian Origen mentions as being older than the Gospel of Luke and was (according to Origen) authentic scripture in the Church of his day.[8] Likewise, some non-Mormon scholars believe that the Nag Hammadi's Gospel of Thomas (although compiled in about AD 140) includes traditions and teachings which are as old as or older than the gospels of Mark, Matthew, Luke, and John.[9]

Categories

With the exception of the letters of the Apostolic Fathers and the writings of the early Christians and historians, most of these recently discovered or rediscovered manuscripts (including the writings from Qumran and Nag Hammadi) fall into one of three categories of ancient writ. These categories are 1) Gnostic, 2) Pseudepigrapha, and 3) Apocrypha. All three categories embody works which are considered by many scholars to be equal in importance to the scriptures included in our Bibles today. Likewise all of the above categories contain works which the Primitive Church (either Christian or Jewish) embraced as scripture.

Gnostic

For forty days after Jesus was resurrected, he taught the Apostles "the things pertaining to the kingdom of God" (Acts 1:3). And what do we have of these teachings in the Bible? Practically nothing! A large percent of the recently discovered Christian writings, however, claim to contain those lost teachings which the Lord conveyed to his disciples following his resurrection. These writings have been dubbed the "forty day literature" by the some scholars. Many of the Nag Hammadi writings are of this nature, and therefore manifest the importance of these ancient texts. These writings are full of doctrines which claim to have come from what Christ taught after his resurrection, where he had gone after the crucifixion, as well as other secret—or sacred—things pertaining to his Father's kingdom.

Naturally the Twelve Apostles asked Christ where he had gone after his death. Any curious mind would ask the same thing. What is beyond?

What does it look like? Some people think that Christ, immediately following his demise, ascended to heaven. In Luke 23:43, Jesus told the thief on the cross beside him, "Verily I say unto thee, To day shalt thou be with me in paradise." But in the book of John, when Mary Magdalene discovered the resurrected Jesus in the garden, the Lord said, "Touch me not; *for I am not yet ascended to my Father:* but go to my brethren, and say unto them, I ascend unto my Father, and your Father; and to my God, and your God" (20:17; italics added). If Christ had not yet ascended to his Father, where had he been for the three days while his body lay dead? Obviously, "paradise" was somewhere other than heaven. Section 85 helps answer this question.

The Greek Gnosis is translated as "knowledge". It "occurs twenty-seven times in the New Testament," notes Nibley, "and always refers to knowledge that comes by revelation. The oldest Christian definition of the Gnosis (and one consistently ignored by students of Gnosticism) is that it was that knowledge the Lord imparted secretly to Peter, James, and John after the Resurrection, and which they in turn transmitted to the others of the Twelve and to the Seventy."[10]

The Gnosis originally applied to the forty-day teachings of Christ to his disciples. These teachings were sacred, or secret, and were not revealed to the general membership of the Church (see Section 83). When the Apostles died, the true Gnosis died off with them. Suddenly a group of mystics—who called themselves Gnostics—sprang up claiming to have the sacred Gnosis. Right away the Christian bishops wrote letters condemning these mystical Gnostics, claiming that they had a false gnosis whereas the Christians retained the true gnosis.[11]

Scholars used to label as "Gnostic" anything they thought was mystical rather than genuinely Christian, but recent scholarship reveals that a real gnosis did exist and that many ideas contained within writings, which were once labeled "Gnostic" (mystical Gnostic), actually demonstrate authentic Christian teachings. Some ideas once labeled "Gnostic" are found in the New Testament and in other orthodox Christian writings. In 1934 eminent scholar Walter Bauer wrote, "Perhaps—certain manifestations of Christian life that the authors of the church renounce as 'heresies' originally had not been such at all, but, at least here and there, were the only forms of the new religion; that is, for those regions, they were simply 'Christianity.' "[12]

Many Gnostic writings were highly prized by the first Christians but when the Church closed the canon of scripture, those books that didn't fit the newly forming "orthodoxy" were purged in the process.

Does this mean that everything contained in these Gnostic writings is true? Should they be considered scripture? The answer is no. Some Gnostic texts encapsulate bits of truth and provide us with valuable insights to Christian teachings which were later lost. But they also contain errors, interpolations, and mystical claptrap that run contrary to what we find in the New Testament and writings of early Churchmen. Early Gnosticism, and some of the later remnants of this group did, however, imitate many "authentic" Christian teachings. Most scholars recognize that many Gnostic ideas were based on models of authentic Christianity. As Nibley explains,

> If one makes a sketch of a mountain, what is it? A few lines on a piece of paper. But there is a solid reality behind this poor composition; even if the tattered scrap is picked up later in a street in Tokyo or a gutter in Madrid, it still attests to the artist's experience of the mountain as a reality. If the sketch should be copied by others who have never seen the original mountain, it still bears witness to its reality. So it is with the apocryphal [and Gnostic] writings: most of them are pretty poor stuff and all of them are copies of copies. But when we compare them we cannot escape the impression that they have a real model behind them, more faithfully represented in some than in others. All we get on this earth, Paul reminds us, is a distorted reflection, but it is a reflection of things that really are.[13]

Some debate still exists concerning which so-called Gnostic teachings are early orthodox Christian teachings, and which are the later innovations of the mystics. Those teachings that are supported by early Christian bishops, historians, other writings, and New Testament authors are more likely to be accurate in describing authentic Christian doctrines.

But what did Joseph Smith know about these Gnostic texts? Elaine Pagels, author of *The Gnostic Gospels,* says that of the handful of Gnostic texts known to scholars, "none" had been "published before the nineteenth century."[14] Even if a few were available to Joseph, we'd have to show that they were available to Joseph and that he had studied their contents.

Pseudepigrapha

Pseude and *pigrapha* literally means "uncertain writings." A pseude-pigraphical book is a work which was written by an author under an assumed name (pseudonym), or the name of some other well-known author.[15] Most scholars believe that several books of the Old Testament—including certain chapters of Zechariah and Isaiah—were written pseudonymously. Some pseudepigraphic books are simply copies of copies of books which were originally written by their claimed authors. In this sense much of the Book of Mormon could be considered pseudepigrapha. Mormon condensed and abridged writings which were under the names of different authors or prophets.

Because many pseudepigraphical books were found among the Dead Sea Scrolls, scholars now believe that these writings hold a place of importance so far denied them. Reverend Dr. James H. Charlesworth, director of Duke University International Center for the Study of Christian Origins, says: "Many of the long overlooked documents could have fittingly been included in the Bible itself and were considered equally inspired by first-century Christians and Jews. A lot of specialists now think they should have been included. They're Biblical books and they're going to be recognized as supplements to the Bible, to be studied with the Holy Bible."[16]

It's likely that Jesus was familiar with some of the Pseudepigrapha. The Book of Enoch, for example, influenced nearly all New Testament authors (especially Jude) and is quoted at least 128 times in the New Testament.[17]

This is especially interesting because from June 1830 until February 1831, Joseph Smith received revelations, which he entitled, "Extracts from the Prophecy of Enoch." It wasn't until 1882, however, before the first translation of Enoch was published in the United States.[18] Many of the things found in the various versions of the ancient book of Enoch, are also found in the revelations of Joseph Smith (see sections 81 and 84).

Apocrypha

Apocrypha means "hidden or secret writings." Catholic Bibles include the Apocrypha but they had not really drawn the attention of scholars until the middle of the twentieth century when some apocryphal books were discovered among the Dead Sea Scrolls.

The classification of which books are Apocrypha and which are not is confusing and is debated hotly among scholars. No two lists of Apocryphal books are the same. The early Christians, notes Nibley, "made no distinction whatever between canonical books and Apocrypha. . . . The idea of Canon vs. Apocrypha is an invention or rather a convention of scholarship."[19]

By at least 1833, Joseph Smith was aware of the Apocrypha and he asked the Lord about them. He was told that while many things in the Apocrypha were true, they did contain errors and interpolations and it wasn't necessary that he should retranslate them. The Lord suggested that those who were interested in the Apocrypha should read them under the direction of the Spirit and they would be benefitted (see D&C 91).

A modern study of the Apocrypha, however, sometimes adds support to unique LDS teachings. While it could be argued that Joseph gleaned material from the Apocrypha before translating the Book of Mormon, it must be remembered that Joseph's question to the Lord about the Apocrypha took place nearly four years after he finished the Book of Mormon. It should also be remembered that Joseph dictated the Nephite records in about seventy-five days, never read any portions back, and did not rely on notes or books during the dictating process. The likelihood that Joseph utilized any material from the Apocrypha diminishes to an unrealistic status when we account for what we know about Joseph before and during the translating process.

NOTES

1. O. Preston Robinson and Christine H. Robinson, *Christ's Eternal Gospel* (Salt Lake City, UT: Deseret Book, 1976), 55.
2. Mattson, *The Dead Sea Scrolls*, 11–12.
3. James L. Barker, *Apostasy from the Divine Church* (Salt Lake City, UT: Bookcraft, 1960), 19–20.
4. Ibid., 52.
5. Pagels, *The Gnostic Gospels*, xi–xii; see also Mattson, 39.
6. Pagles, *The Gnostic Gospels*, xviii.

7. S. Kent Brown and C. Wilfred Griggs, "The Messiah and the Manuscripts," *Ensign,* Sept. 1974, 72.
8. Nibley, *Since Cumorah,* 49.
9. Pagles, *The Gnostic Gospels,* xv–xvi.
10. Nibley, *Since Cumorah,* 82.
11. Nibley, *The World and the Prophets,* 65.
12. Pagels, *The Gnostic Gospels,* xxxiii.
13. Nibley, *Nibley on the Timely and the Timeless,* 40.
14. Pagels, *The Gnostic Gospels,* xxiv.
15. Robinson and Robinson, *Christ's Eternal Gospel,* 95.
16. Mattson, *The Dead Sea Scrolls,* 136–37.
17. Hugh Nibley, "Enoch the Prophet," *Enoch the Prophet,* 8.
18. Nibley, "A Strange Thing in the Land," *Enoch the Prophet,* 107.
19. Nibley, *Since Cumorah,* 38.

ABOUT THE AUTHOR

*M*ichael R. Ash is the owner and operator of Mormon-Fortress.com and is on the management team for the *Foundation of Apologetic Information and Research* (FAIRLDS.org). He has been published in *Sunstone, Dialogue: A Journal of Mormon Thought,* the Maxwell Institute's *FARMS Review,* and is the author of *Shaken Faith Syndrome: Strengthening One's Testimony in the Face of Criticism and Doubt.*

He and his wife live in Ogden, Utah, and have three daughters and four grandchildren.